GoodFood
101 Slow-cooking recipes

10 9 8 7 6 5 4 3 2 1

Published in 2010 by BBC Books, an imprint of Ebury Publishing
A Random House Group company

The Random House Group Limited
Reg. No. 954009

Addresses for companies within the Random House Group can be found at www.randomhouse.co.uk

A CIP catalogue record for this book is available from the British Library

The Random House Group Limited supports The Forest Stewardship Council (FSC), the leading international forest certification organization. All our titles that are printed on Greenpeace approved FSC certified paper carry the FSC logo. Our paper procurement policy can be found at www.rbooks.co.uk/environment

To buy books by your favourite authors and register for offers visit www.rbooks.co.uk

Printed and bound by Firmengruppe APPL, aprinta druck, Wemding, Germany
Colour origination by Dot Gradations Ltd, UK

Commissioning Editor: Muna Reyal
Project Editor: Joe Cottington
Designer: Annette Peppis
Production: David Brimble
Picture Researcher: Gabby Harrington

ISBN: 9781849901116

Picture credits

BBC *Good Food* magazine and BBC Books would like to thank the following people for providing photos. While every effort has been made to trace and acknowledge all photographers, we should like to apologise should there be any errors or omissions.

Marie-Louise Avery p97, p211; Steve Baxter p49; Peter Cassidy p19, p21, p39, p109, p129; Jean Cazals p33, p81, p83, p111, p181; Ken Field p115, p127; Tim Imrie p207; Dave King p79; Lisa Linder p71; William Lingwood p69, p101, p143, p185, p209; Gareth Morgans p135; David Munns p51, p55, p89, p93, p119, p137, p141, p167, p169, p177, p193; Myles New p31, p65, p155, p163, p183; Lis Parsons p47, p53, p67, p75, p125, p131, p145, p197; Craig Robertson p29, p107; Maja Smend p123, p191; Simon Smith p117; Roger Stowell p63, p133, p173, p175; Sam Stowell p113; Yuki Sugiura p13, p27; Martin Thompson p95; Debi Treloar p73, p87, p157, p159, p201; Trevor Vandial p205; Simon Walton p61; Cameron Watt p15, p23, p77, p99, p103, p165; Philip Webb p11, p17, p41, p59, p105, p149, p151, p153, p171, p179, p187, p189, p199, p203; Simon Wheeler p25, p35, p37, p147, p195; Kate Whitaker p43; Geoff Wilkinson p91, p161; Tim Young p45; Elizabeth Zeschin p57

All the recipes in this book were created by the editorial team at *Good Food* and by regular contributors to BBC Magazines.

GoodFood
101 Slow-cooking recipes

Editor **Sharon Brown**

Contents

Introduction

Slow cooking is a great way to cook all kinds of dishes, from stews and casseroles to scrummy steamed puds. Most of these recipes take just minutes to prepare, then can be left to cook while you get on with other things as your kitchen fills with delicious aromas, leaving you to anticipate the wonderful supper to come.

Slow cooking can save you money, too, as it's the best way to cook those cheaper cuts of meat that had been long-since forgotten and can now be found on every top chef's restaurant menu – such as belly of pork, braising beef and lamb shoulder. These cuts need long, slow cooking to produce meltingly soft, full-flavoured meat cooked to perfection in its own juices.

In this collection we've taken 101 of *Good Food* magazine's favourite slow-cooked recipes. There are a host of main-course dishes, including one-pots, ideas for vegetarians and family favourites, and there's also a chapter of easy slow-cooked methods for many people's best get-together meal of the week – the Sunday roast. Just try *Roast pork with jerk spices* (see page 108) or *Catalan chicken with white wine juices* (see page 94) for a whole new Sunday-lunch experience.

Slow-cooked dishes are great for any occasion – from family suppers to dinner-party dishes – and, as always, all the recipes here have been tried and triple-tested in the *Good Food* kitchen.

Sharon

Sharon Brown
Good Food magazine

Notes and conversion tables

NOTES ON THE RECIPES
• Eggs are large in the UK and Australia and extra large in America unless stated otherwise.
• Wash fresh produce before preparation.
• Recipes contain nutritional analyses for 'sugar', which means the total sugar content including all natural sugars in the ingredients, unless otherwise stated.

OVEN TEMPERATURES

Gas	°C	°C Fan	°F	Oven temp.
¼	110	90	225	Very cool
½	120	100	250	Very cool
1	140	120	275	Cool or slow
2	150	130	300	Cool or slow
3	160	140	325	Warm
4	180	160	350	Moderate
5	190	170	375	Moderately hot
6	200	180	400	Fairly hot
7	220	200	425	Hot
8	230	210	450	Very hot
9	240	220	475	Very hot

APPROXIMATE WEIGHT CONVERSIONS
• All the recipes in this book list both imperial and metric measurements. Conversions are approximate and have been rounded up or down. Follow one set of measurements only; do not mix the two.
• Cup measurements, which are used by cooks in Australia and America, have not been listed here as they vary from ingredient to ingredient. Kitchen scales should be used to measure dry/solid ingredients.

Good Food is concerned about sustainable sourcing and animal welfare. Where possible, humanely reared meats, sustainably caught fish (see fishonline.org for further information from the Marine Conservation Society) and free-range chickens and eggs are used when recipes are originally tested.

SPOON MEASURES

Spoon measurements are level unless otherwise specified.

- 1 teaspoon (tsp) = 5ml
- 1 tablespoon (tbsp) = 15ml
- 1 Australian tablespoon = 20ml (cooks in Australia should measure 3 teaspoons where 1 tablespoon is specified in a recipe)

APPROXIMATE LIQUID CONVERSIONS

metric	imperial	AUS	US
50ml	2fl oz	¼ cup	¼ cup
125ml	4fl oz	½ cup	½ cup
175ml	6fl oz	¾ cup	¾ cup
225ml	8fl oz	1 cup	1 cup
300ml	10fl oz/½ pint	½ pint	1¼ cups
450ml	16fl oz	2 cups	2 cups/1 pint
600ml	20fl oz/1 pint	1 pint	2½ cups
1 litre	35fl oz/1¾ pints	1¾ pints	1 quart

Salt beef with beetroot & horseradish relish

Simmering the beef gently in this recipe gives a meltingly tender result. The fiery beetroot relish is also wonderful served sparingly with smoked fish.

TAKES 2½ HOURS • SERVES 6

1.5kg/3lb 5oz piece salted brisket or silverside of beef
1 large onion, halved
large bunch of fresh parsley
6 young carrots, scrubbed and left whole
6 small leeks

FOR THE RELISH

3 large home-cooked beetroot, coarsely grated
3 tbsp freshly grated horseradish
2 tsp golden caster sugar
2 tbsp balsamic vinegar

1 Put the beef in a pan that is big enough to fit it and all the vegetables. Cover it with water and bring to the boil, skimming off the froth that comes to the surface. Tip the onion and parsley into the pan and simmer gently for 1 hour, skimming as necessary. Add the carrots and simmer for 30 minutes. Finally, add the leeks and simmer for 30 minutes longer. The meat is ready when it feels tender when prodded with a fork.

2 While the meat cooks, mix the beetroot and horseradish with the sugar and vinegar until the sugar has dissolved.

3 Remove the beef from the pan and put it on a serving dish, then scoop out the carrots and leeks, and add to the beef. Slice the beef and serve with the vegetables and relish – but warn everyone that a little of the hot relish goes a long way! You can also offer some cooking liquid to drizzle over if anyone wants it.

PER SERVING 542 kcals, protein 50g, carbs 21g, fat 30g, sat fat 13g, fibre 6g, sugar 19g, salt 4.14g

Boston baked beans

This is perfect family fare that the kids will love. Haricot beans take very well to the sweetly spiced flavours of this dish.

TAKES 2½–3 HOURS, PLUS SOAKING
● **SERVES 6**

500g pack dried haricot beans
2 onions, roughly chopped
2 celery sticks, roughly chopped
2 carrots, roughly chopped
2 tbsp Dijon mustard
2 tbsp light muscovado sugar
½ tbsp black treacle or molasses
2 tbsp tomato purée
800g/1lb 12oz piece belly pork
handful of fresh parsley, roughly
   chopped, to garnish

1 Soak the beans in a large bowl of cold water for at least 4 hours or overnight. Heat oven to 180C/160C fan/gas 4. Drain and rinse the beans, and put in a large flameproof casserole with 1.5 litres/ 2½ pints water. Boil for 10 minutes, skimming off any froth that appears on the surface.

2 Add the onions, celery, carrots, mustard, sugar, treacle or molasses and tomato purée. Stir until everything is well mixed, then bury the piece of pork in among the beans. Cover tightly and cook in the oven for 2–2½ hours until the beans and pork are very tender. Check halfway through the cooking time and top up with hot water from the kettle if necessary.

3 Take the pork out of the pot. Cut into large chunks and serve with the beans, sprinkled with parsley.

PER SERVING 615 kcals, protein 43g, carbs 54g, fat 27g, sat fat 10g, fibre 16g, sugar 14g, salt 0.8g

Chicken with chunky vegetables

Braising the chicken slowly with vegetables in a casserole dish gives a tender, juicy result. A whole chicken makes a stunning centrepiece to bring to the table.

TAKES 1½ HOURS • SERVES 4

2 tbsp olive oil
250g/9oz shallots, peeled
8 small carrots, peeled and halved
2 sticks celery, cut into 5cm/2in lengths
2 leeks, cut into 5cm/2in lengths
1 chicken (about 1.5kg/3lb 5oz),
    preferably free-range
425ml/¾ pint each chicken stock and
    dry white wine
2 bay leaves
2 sprigs thyme
2 parsley stalks

1 Heat oven to 180C/160C fan/gas 4. Heat 1 tablespoon of the oil in a large frying pan and cook the shallots over a medium heat until just beginning to brown. Add the remaining vegetables and cook for 5 minutes until just golden. Using a slotted spoon remove from the pan and set aside.

2 Add the remaining oil to pan and brown the chicken well on all sides. Place the chicken in a large pot with a tight-fitting lid. Pour any excess fat out of the frying pan and return to the hob. Deglaze the pan with the stock and wine, scraping up the crispy bits.

3 Arrange the shallots and uncooked vegetables around the chicken and pour over the wine and stock. Tuck the herbs around the chicken, season, cover with a lid and cook for 1 hour 10 minutes or until the juices run clear. Remove the lid for the final 15 minutes to further brown the chicken.

PER SERVING 663 kcals, protein 52g, carbs 10g, fat 39g, sat fat 10g, fibre 4g, sugar none, salt 1g

Beef in stout with thyme dumplings

A long-standing Irish favourite; adding chestnuts gives the dish a nutty flavour, and the herb dumplings are cooked uncovered to give them lovely crusty tops.

TAKES 3¼ HOURS ● SERVES 6

1 tbsp seasoned plain flour
1.25kg/2lb 12oz stewing beef, cut into
   4cm/1½in chunks
3 tbsp oil
2 onions, finely sliced
1 celery stick, chopped
425ml/¾ pint stout
2 tsp light muscovado sugar
1 tbsp tomato purée
1 tbsp Worcestershire sauce
1 bouquet garni
100g/4oz self-raising flour
2 tsp chopped fresh thyme leaves
2 tsp mustard seeds
50g/2oz butter, frozen in foil
250g/9oz cooked and peeled chestnuts

1 Heat oven to 160C/140C fan/gas 3. Put the plain flour in a plastic bag, add the beef and shake well.

2 Heat 2 tablespoons of the oil in a large flameproof casserole, fry the onions for 7 minutes, then remove. Add the remaining oil, then stir-fry the beef until sealed all over. Return the onions to the pan with the celery, stout, 150ml/¼ pint water, sugar, purée, Worcestershire sauce and bouquet garni. Bring to the boil, scraping up any bits. Season, cover, and cook in the oven for 2 hours.

3 About 10 minutes before the end of the cooking time, put the self-raising flour, thyme and mustard seeds in a bowl and season. Grate in the frozen butter and mix well. Gradually stir in 2–3 tablespoons cold water to form a soft dough. Shape into 12 balls.

4 Stir the chestnuts into the beef casserole and put the dumplings on top. Cook, uncovered, for 20–25 minutes.

PER SERVING 598 kcals, protein 49g, carbs 40g, fat 26g, sat fat 10g, fibre 3g, sugar none, salt 0.82g

Crisp Chinese pork

Without the dipping sauce this recipe is essentially two ingredients – it couldn't be easier, and you get perfect crackling and melt-in-the-mouth meat.

TAKES ABOUT 2¼ HOURS, PLUS SALTING • SERVES 4

1.3kg/3lb piece boned pork belly, skin on and scored (ask the butcher for the thin end)

2 tsp Chinese five spice powder

boiled rice and steamed greens, to serve (optional)

FOR THE DIPPING SAUCE

4 tbsp soy sauce

small thumb-sized piece of ginger, grated

1 tbsp Thai sweet chilli sauce

1 spring onion, finely chopped

1 Rub the pork with the five spice and 2 teaspoons sea salt then leave, uncovered, in the fridge for at least 2 hours, but preferably overnight.

2 When ready to cook, heat oven to its maximum setting. Lay the pork on a rack over a roasting tin, making sure the skin is exposed. Roast for 10 minutes before turning down the heat to 180C/160C fan/gas 4, then leave to cook for a further 1½ hours. Have a look at the pork – if the skin isn't crisp, turn up the heat to 220C/200C fan/gas 7 and cook for another 30 minutes until crisp. Leave to rest on a board for at least 10 minutes.

3 To make the dipping sauce, mix all the ingredients together in a bowl with 2 tablespoons water. Cut the pork into small pieces, then serve with the sauce, plus boiled rice and steamed greens, if you like.

PER SERVING 696 kcals, protein 59g, carbs 3g, fat 50g, sat fat 19g, fibre none, sugar 2g, salt 5.83g

Texan chilli with baked potatoes

Chipotle, a smoked jalapeño chilli, often comes in an adobo sauce – a spicy blend of chillies, herbs and vinegar. Use it sparingly as the piquant flavour packs a real punch.

TAKES 1 HOUR • SERVES 4

4 baking potatoes
1 tbsp olive oil
450g/1lb lean minced beef
1 red onion, finely chopped
1 red pepper, seeded and chopped
1 tbsp ground cumin
2 tbsp tomato purée
½ chipotle chilli in adobo sauce, finely
    chopped
350ml/12fl oz hot vegetable stock
400g can black or kidney beans,
    drained and rinsed
low-fat plain yogurt and grated low-fat
    Cheddar, to serve

1 Heat oven to 220C/200C fan/gas 7. Put the potatoes on a baking sheet and cook for 1 hour until softened.

2 Meanwhile, heat the oil in a large, non-stick frying pan and fry the beef, onion and pepper for about 10 minutes over a medium–high heat until golden and browned. Stir through the cumin, tomato purée and chipotle, and cook for 1 minute more. Pour over the vegetable stock and leave to simmer for around 20 minutes, then add the beans and cook for 5 minutes more until they have warmed through.

3 Split the potatoes, spoon over some chilli and serve with the yogurt and Cheddar, if you like.

PER SERVING 478 kcals, protein 36g, carbs 52g, fat 16g, sat fat 5g, fibre 7g, sugar none, salt 1.33g

Pork chops in cider with apples

Chops are ideal for slow braising, but use a shallow dish so the meat doesn't cook in its steam. Sage and apples are traditional partners to pork.

TAKES 1½ HOURS ● SERVES 4

4 × 175g/6oz pork chops
1 tbsp seasoned plain flour
1 tbsp olive oil
1 tsp butter
2 small apples, try Braeburn or Cox's,
    cored and each cut into 8 wedges
250ml/9fl oz dry cider
1 tbsp chopped fresh sage
100ml/3½fl oz double cream
1 tsp wholegrain mustard

1 Heat oven to 160C/140C fan/gas 3. Dust the chops in the seasoned flour. Heat the oil and butter in a frying pan over a high heat and brown the chops on both sides, then transfer them to a shallow ovenproof dish.

2 Add the apples to the frying pan and cook until golden, then remove and add to the chops.

3 Pour the cider into the pan and bring to the boil, scraping any bits from the bottom of the pan. Pour over the chops, season, and cover with foil. Cook in the oven for 45 minutes–1 hour, until the pork is tender.

4 Transfer the pork and apples to a serving plate and keep warm. Put the braising liquid back on the hob, add the sage and cook for about 5 minutes until reduced by almost half. Take the pan off the heat, stir in the cream and mustard, then simmer, stirring, until thickened slightly. Pour over the pork and serve.

PER SERVING 613 kcals, protein 29g, carbs 10g, fat 49g, sat fat 21g, fibre 1g, sugar none, salt 0.3g

Braised beef with red wine & cranberry

This lovely seasonal dish can be left to bubble away, filling the kitchen with comforting aromas. You can make it a couple of days ahead and it will taste even better.

TAKES 2 HOURS • SERVES 4

1kg/2lb 4oz braising steak
2 tbsp seasoned plain flour
2–3 tbsp olive oil
3 onions, thinly sliced
300ml/½ pint red wine
300ml/½ pint stock
3 rounded tbsp cranberry sauce
a handful of flatleaf parsley leaves,
    to garnish
mashed potatoes, to serve

1 Cut the meat into large slices about 8cm square. Tip the seasoned flour into a large food bag, add the beef and shake to coat the pieces.

2 Heat 2 tablespoons of the oil in a large heavy-based pan. Add the beef and fry until evenly browned. (You may need to do this in two batches.) Remove to a plate.

3 Heat the remaining tablespoon of oil in the pan, if you need it, then fry the onions quickly for 5 minutes until tinged brown. Return the beef to the pan and add the wine and stock. Bring to the boil, stirring to scrape up the juices, and season. Reduce the heat, cover tightly with a lid and cook at a gentle simmer for 1½ hours until the beef is tender.

4 Stir in the cranberry sauce. Simmer for a further 5 minutes, then serve with mash and a scattering of parsley.

PER SERVING 481 kcals, protein 57g, carbs 19g, fat 15g, sat fat 6g, fibre 1g, sugar 4g, salt 0.92g

One-pot chicken with braised vegetables

Chicken is always popular with the family. Use fresh peas if they're available, but frozen work just as well. You can use chicken stock instead of the white wine.

TAKES ABOUT 1¾ HOURS

● **SERVES 4**

1 chicken (about 1.5kg/3lb 5oz), preferably free-range

25g/1oz butter

200g/8oz smoked bacon, preferably from a whole piece, cut into small chunks

1kg/2lb 4oz new potatoes, peeled

16–20 shallots or small onions

½ × 75cl bottle white wine

250g/9oz peas, frozen are fine

bunch of fresh soft green herbs, such as tarragon, chives or parsley, chopped

1 Heat oven to 220C/200C fan/gas 7. Season the chicken inside and out with salt and black pepper. Heat the butter in an ovenproof casserole dish until sizzling, then brown the chicken on all sides – this should take about 10 minutes. Remove the chicken from the dish, then fry the bacon until crisp. Add the potatoes and shallots, and cook until just starting to brown. Nestle the chicken among the veg, pour over the wine, then cook, undisturbed, for 1 hour or until the chicken is cooked.

2 After 1 hour, remove the chicken and keep it warm. Return the casserole to the heat and stir the peas into the buttery juices, adding a splash of water if the pan is dry. Simmer until the peas are cooked through. Finally, add any juices from the rested chicken, then stir through the herbs and serve with the chicken.

PER SERVING 915 kcals, protein 63g, carbs 52g, fat 49g, sat fat 17g, fibre 6g, sugar 10g, salt 2.58g

Moroccan lamb with apricots & almonds

This full-of-flavour fruity casserole is great served with couscous and is special enough for a casual supper with friends.

TAKES 2 HOURS • SERVES 4

2 tbsp olive oil
550g/1lb 4oz lean lamb, cubed
1 onion, chopped
2 garlic cloves, crushed
700ml/1¼ pints lamb or chicken stock
grated zest and juice of 1 orange
1 cinnamon stick
1 tsp clear honey
175g/6oz ready-to-eat dried apricots
3 tbsp chopped fresh mint
25g/1oz ground almonds
25g/1oz toasted flaked almonds
steamed broccoli and couscous,
    to serve

1 Heat the oil in a large flameproof casserole dish. Add the lamb and cook over a medium-high heat for around 3–4 minutes until evenly browned, stirring often. Remove the lamb to a plate using a slotted spoon.

2 Stir the onion and garlic into the casserole, and cook gently for 5 minutes until softened. Return the lamb to the pot. Add the stock, zest and juice, cinnamon, honey and salt and black pepper. Bring to the boil then reduce the heat, cover, and cook gently for 1 hour.

3 Add the apricots and two-thirds of the mint and cook for 30 minutes until the lamb is tender. Stir in the ground almonds to thicken the sauce. Scatter over the remaining mint and the toasted almonds, and serve with broccoli and couscous on the side.

PER SERVING 441 kcals, protein 38g, carbs 5g, fat 21g, sat fat 7g, fibre 1g, sugar 3g, salt 2g

Summer daube of beef

This dish can be made ahead and stored in the fridge for up to 2 days. Simply reheat on the hob for 25–30 minutes.

TAKES 3½ HOURS • SERVES 4–6

1–1.5kg/2.4–3.5lb topside of beef
2 tbsp olive oil
100g/4oz unsmoked bacon, chopped, or lardons
2 garlic cloves, chopped or crushed
600ml/1 pint white wine
large fresh thyme sprig, leaves stripped, or 1 tsp dried
400g can chopped tomatoes
4 ripe tomatoes, chopped
4 carrots, peeled and sliced
3 tbsp pitted black olives

1 Heat oven to 160C/140C fan/gas 3. Season the meat all over, then heat the oil in a large, heavy flameproof casserole. Fry the meat until browned all over, add the bacon or lardons and fry until lightly coloured. Stir in the garlic, wine, thyme, canned tomatoes and some seasoning. Bring to the boil, then reduce the heat to a simmer and cover tightly with a lid. If your lid is not tightly fitted, put a sheet of foil between the casserole and lid and scrunch up the edges.

2 Transfer to the oven and cook for 2 hours. Stir in the fresh tomatoes, carrots and olives and return to the oven for 1 hour until the meat is very tender. Serve immediately.

PER SERVING (6) 502 kcals, protein 38g, carbs 13g, fat 30g, sat fat 12g, fibre 3g, sugar 12g, salt 1.03g

Chicken with braised celery & cider

Cooking the chicken upside down first keeps the breast moist and succulent.
Serve with new potatoes and steamed broccoli.

TAKES 1 HOUR 40 MINUTES
● **SERVES 4**

small knob of butter
1 chicken (about 2kg/4lb 8oz),
    preferably free-range
4 rashers smoked streaky bacon,
    chopped
1 onion, finely chopped
2 carrots, diced
1 fresh thyme sprig
2 celery hearts, quartered
150ml/¼ pint dry cider
300ml/½ pint chicken stock

1 Heat oven to 190C/170C fan/gas 5. Heat the butter in a large casserole dish and brown the chicken slowly on all sides; this should take a good 10–15 minutes. (Be patient, it will pay off later.)
2 Take the chicken out of the dish, throw in the bacon and cook for 3–4 minutes until starting to crisp, then add the onion, carrots and thyme and continue to cook for 4–5 minutes until the vegetables soften. Stir the celery into the dish, then nestle the chicken among the veg, breast-side down. Pour over the cider and stock, bring to a simmer, then cook the chicken, uncovered, for 1 hour.
3 Turn the chicken the right way up and give it 30 minutes more, by which point the legs should be coming away. Carefully lift the chicken from the dish. Check the seasoning of the vegetables and serve with the chicken.

PER SERVING 679 kcals, protein 62g, carbs 7g, fat 44g, sat fat 14g, fibre 2g, sugar 6g, salt 1.37g

Slow-cooked lamb with onions & thyme

This simple one-pot makes a great winter supper. The slow cooking provides a deeply satisfying exchange of flavours. Serve with plenty of creamy mash and broccoli.

TAKES 3½ HOURS • SERVES 4

½ leg of lamb (about 1.25kg/2lb 12oz)
3 tbsp olive oil
1kg/2lb 4oz onions (about 4 large ones)
handful of fresh thyme sprigs
300ml/½ pint red wine
large handful of fresh parsley

1 Heat oven to 160C/140C fan/gas 3. Wipe the meat all over and season well. Heat the oil in a large, heavy flameproof casserole with a tight-fitting lid, add the meat and fry it all over on a fairly high heat for about 8 minutes, turning it until it is evenly well browned. Remove to a plate.

2 Thinly slice the onions, then add them to the pan and fry for about 10 minutes, until softened and brown-tinged. Add a few of the thyme sprigs and cook for a further minute or so. Season with salt and black pepper.

3 Sit the lamb on top of the onions, then add the wine. Cover with the lid and bake for 3 hours. (You can make to this stage up to 2 days in advance, then reheat for 45 minutes in the oven.)

4 To finish off, strip the leaves from 2 more thyme sprigs and chop them with the parsley. Scatter over before serving.

PER SERVING 731 kcals, protein 63g, carbs 21g, fat 39g, sat fat 19g, fibre 4g, sugar none, salt 0.87g

Chilli con carne soup

This is a mellow, soupy version of a classic chilli. The chocolate gives a delicious depth of flavour.

TAKES 1½ HOURS • SERVES 6

1 small onion, finely chopped
2 garlic cloves, finely chopped
1 tbsp vegetable oil
500g/1lb 2oz lean minced beef
410g can pinto or red kidney beans, drained and rinsed
2 × 400g cans chopped plum tomatoes
700ml/1¼ pints hot chicken stock
large pinch of crushed dried chillies
2 squares dark chocolate
fresh coriander or parsley leaves and grated Gruyère, to garnish

1 Gently fry the onion and garlic in the oil in a large pan for a couple of minutes until beginning to soften, then add the mince. Raise the heat and cook for around 5 minutes, stirring from time to time, until the meat is no longer pink.

2 Stir in the beans, tomatoes, stock, chillies, chocolate and plenty of salt and black pepper. Bring to the boil, cover, and simmer very gently for 1 hour, or longer if you have the time. (You can make it up to a day ahead to this point, then cool and chill.)

3 Ladle into mugs or large cups and scatter with herbs, cheese and black pepper. (You'll need spoons to eat it.)

PER SERVING 252 kcals, protein 24g, carbs 14g, fat 12g, sat fat 5g, fibre 4g, sugar 1g, salt 1.29g

Beef pie with crisp potato crust

Here's a new style of pie that all the family will love. The grated potato makes a really light, healthy and delicious topping.

TAKES ABOUT 2¾ HOURS • SERVES 4

1 tbsp olive oil

500g/1lb 2oz beef braising steak, cut into chunks

1 onion, roughly chopped

250g pack oyster mushrooms, sliced if large

1 tbsp tomato purée

1 tbsp flour

100ml/3½fl oz red wine

200ml/7fl oz hot beef stock, from a cube

350g/12oz potatoes, peeled

25g/1oz butter, chopped into small pieces

1 Heat the oil in a non-stick pan over a high heat. Add the beef and cook for 10 minutes until browned all over, then remove from the pan. Fry the onion for 7 minutes until softened, then stir through the mushrooms and cook for 3 minutes more until golden. Stir in the tomato purée and flour, and cook for 1 minute more.

2 Pour in the wine and beef stock, and bring to a simmer. Return the beef to the pan and cook, uncovered, over a gentle heat for 2 hours until the meat is really tender, topping up with water, if needed. Pour all of the mixture into a 2-litre baking dish.

3 Heat oven to 190C/170C fan/gas 5. Boil the potatoes for 10 minutes until beginning to soften. Cool under a running tap, then coarsely grate them over the beef. Dot the top with butter, then pop the dish in the oven and cook for 30 minutes until the crust is nice and crispy.

PER SERVING 386 kcals, protein 30g, carbs 21g, fat 19g, sat fat 8g, fibre 2g, sugar none, salt 0.66g

Chinese braised pork with spring onions

Fresh ginger, spring onion, chilli and soy sauce combine here for the familiar flavours of the East, and the slow cooking adds tenderness to the pork.

TAKES 2¾ HOURS • **SERVES 4**

1 tbsp oil
4 pork osso bucco pieces (about 850g/1lb 14oz) or the equivalent of pork shoulder
250ml/9fl oz Shaohsing rice wine or dry sherry
100g/4oz ginger, finely sliced
2 garlic cloves, sliced
12 spring onions (8 fat ones and 4 thinner ones)
1 dried red chilli
500ml/18fl oz chicken or vegetable stock
1 tbsp miso paste (optional)
2 tbsp soy sauce
steamed rice and bok choy, to serve

1 Heat oven to 190C/170C fan/gas 5. Heat the oil in a large frying pan and brown the pork on both sides, then transfer it to a large casserole dish. Deglaze the pan you used for browning with the rice wine or sherry, and add it to the casserole. Add the ginger and garlic. Trim the ends off the 8 fat spring onions and add these to the pan, whole, along with the chilli, stock, miso paste (if using) and soy sauce. Bring everything to a simmer, then cover and cook in the oven for 2 hours.

2 Remove the lid from the casserole and cook for a further 20 minutes. Chop the 4 thinner spring onions and add them to the casserole just before serving with steamed rice and bok choy.

PER SERVING 392 kcals, protein 38g, carbs 5g, fat 21g, sat fat 7g, fibre 1g, sugar 3g, salt 2g

Boiled bacon with cabbage & carrots

An old-fashioned favourite that's always worth revisiting. Use the leftover stock to make a hearty broth with shredded cabbage, lentils and chunks of leftover bacon.

TAKES 2 HOURS ● SERVES 6

1.3kg/3lb piece smoked bacon
1 onion, peeled and studded with
   6 cloves
large bunch of fresh herbs tied
   together, including bay, thyme and
   parsley stalks
1 bunch new-season carrots (about
   12 in total), scrubbed and trimmed
2 pointed cabbages, trimmed and each
   cut into 6 wedges

FOR THE MUSTARD SAUCE

150ml/¼ pint stock (from cooking the
   bacon)
142ml pot double cream
3 tbsp English mustard
handful of fresh curly parsley leaves,
   chopped

1 Put the bacon in a stockpot with the onion and herbs, then cover with water. Bring to a simmer, then cook for around 45 minutes, topping up with water, if needed. Add the carrots, then continue to cook for 15 minutes. Ladle 150ml/ ¼ pint of the stock into a smaller pan and set aside. Add the cabbage wedges to the stockpot, then continue to cook everything for another 10–15 minutes until the cabbage is nice and tender but not overcooked.

2 Meanwhile, make the sauce. Pour the cream into the reserved stock and bring to the boil. Simmer for a few minutes, then whisk in the mustard and parsley. Season to taste.

3 Remove the meat from the stock, then carve it into thick slices. Serve on a platter with the cabbage and carrots, and moisten with a trickle of stock. Serve the sauce separately.

PER SERVING 694 kcals, protein 36g, carbs 9g, fat 57g, sat fat 23g, fibre 3g, sugar 8g, salt 4.51g

Spiced lamb & squash stew

Harissa is a fiery chilli paste that is widely available in supermarkets in tubes or in jars.
Curry paste is a good alternative if you can't find it, though the taste will be different.

TAKES 2 HOURS • SERVES 4

3 tbsp olive oil

900g/2lb lamb neck fillet, trimmed and
    cut into bite-sized pieces

1 onion, roughly chopped

2 garlic cloves, crushed

2.5cm/1in piece ginger, grated

1 tbsp tomato purée

1 tbsp harissa paste

25g/1oz plain flour

1.2 litres/2 pints lamb stock

1.3kg/3lb butternut squash

4 tomatoes, skinned, seeded and
    roughly chopped

400g can chickpeas, drained and rinsed

225g bag baby leaf spinach

2 tbsp lemon juice

crusty bread, to serve

1 Heat the oil in a large pan, add the lamb and cook over a high heat for 4–5 minutes until browned all over, stirring occasionally. Add the onion, garlic and ginger, and cook for 3–4 minutes until softened. Stir in the tomato purée, harissa and flour, and cook over a medium heat for 1–2 minutes. Pour in the stock, bring to the boil, cover and simmer for 45 minutes.

2 Cut the squash in half and scoop out the seeds. Peel and cut the flesh into bite-sized chunks. Add the tomatoes, squash and chickpeas to the lamb mixture, and cook for 30 minutes, stirring occasionally.

3 Stir in the spinach and lemon juice, and cook for a further 1–2 minutes. Season and serve with crusty bread.

PER SERVING 673 kcals, protein 52g, carbs 45g, fat 33g, sat fat 14g, fibre 10g, sugar none, salt 1.18g

Braised pork with prunes

Don't be put off by the inclusion of prunes – they simply melt away to give a really rich, slightly sweet sauce. Serve with buttered noodles, pasta or mash.

TAKES 2 HOURS • SERVES 4

1 tbsp olive oil

600g/1lb 5oz pork shoulder, roughly cut into 5cm/2in chunks

small knob of butter

1 onion, sliced

1 tbsp plain flour

2 large glasses fruity rosé or white wine

300ml/½ pint chicken stock

140g/5oz dried prunes (about 12)

handful of fresh parsley, chopped, to garnish

1 Heat the oil in a flameproof casserole and cook the pork for about 10 minutes, turning occasionally, until it is golden brown all over. You need plenty of space in the pan, so cook the meat in two batches if it starts to steam. Remove from the pan to a plate. Tip out any burnt bits, then add the butter and cook the onion for 3–5 minutes until softened.

2 Stir in the flour, then return the pork and juices to the pan. Pour over the wine and enough stock to cover the meat. Bring to the boil, reduce to a simmer, put the lid on and cook for 45 minutes, stirring occasionally.

3 Tip in the prunes, top up with more stock or water if the meat isn't covered, and cook for a further 45 minutes or so, uncovered, until really tender. Serve sprinkled with parsley.

PER SERVING 497 kcals, protein 29g, carbs 22g, fat 28g, sat fat 10g, fibre 1g, sugar none, salt 0.54g

Chicken casserole with red wine & peppers

This casserole makes a substantial main course served with creamy mash. It freezes well for up to 2 months; thaw thoroughly overnight and reheat for 45 minutes.

TAKES 1½ HOURS • SERVES 4

2 tbsp olive oil

8 chicken thighs, bone in

1 red pepper, seeded and quartered

1 green pepper, seeded and quartered

2 garlic cloves, finely chopped

1 leek, trimmed and thickly sliced

200g/8oz cooked ham, cut into chunks

1 tsp paprika

300ml/½ pint red wine

400g can chopped tomatoes

1 tbsp tomato purée

2 fresh thyme sprigs or ½ tsp dried

2 tbsp chopped parsley, to garnish

mashed potato, to serve

1 Heat oven to 160C/140C fan/gas 3. Heat the oil in a large flameproof casserole and fry the chicken over a high heat until browned all over. Remove to a plate with a slotted spoon and set aside. Reduce the heat slightly and add the peppers. Cook for 2–3 minutes, turning, until they brown. Add the garlic and leek, cook for 2–3 minutes, then stir in the ham.

2 Sprinkle over the paprika, cook for a couple of seconds, then add the wine and bubble for a few minutes. Return the chicken to the casserole. Tip in the tomatoes, purée and thyme, and mix well. Pour in enough water to just cover the chicken and season. Bring to a simmer, cover and transfer to the oven. Cook for 1 hour, until the sauce thickens and the chicken is tender. Sprinkle over the parsley and serve with mash.

PER SERVING 896 kcals, protein 71g, carbs 9g, fat 59g, sat fat 17g, fibre 3g, sugar none, salt 2.39g

Lamb & apricot hotpot

Once prepared you can leave this hotpot to bubble away in the oven for 2 hours. It can be made earlier in the day or even the day before, as it reheats well.

TAKES 2½ HOURS • SERVES 4

2 tbsp olive oil

3 onions, sliced

2 tsp fresh thyme leaves or 1 tsp dried

2 bay leaves

1kg/2lb 4oz potatoes (Maris Piper are excellent)

700g/1lb 9oz boneless lamb leg or shoulder

175g/6oz ready-to-eat dried apricots

600ml/1 pint vegetable or chicken stock

1 Heat oven to 180C/160C fan/gas 4. Heat the oil in a frying pan, add the onions and fry gently for 10 minutes until they are softened. Add the thyme and bay leaves.

2 Thickly slice the potatoes and arrange a third in the base of a deep, lidded ovenproof dish (about 2-litre capacity). Cut the lamb into large chunks. Put half the lamb on top, then half the onions and apricots and half the remaining potatoes. Repeat this, finishing with a layer of potatoes.

3 Heat the stock and pour it over the hotpot. Cover the dish tightly and bake for 1½ hours, then remove the lid and cook for a further 30 minutes to brown the potatoes. Serve using a large spoon, straight from the dish.

PER SERVING 512 kcals, protein 25g, carbs 68g, fat 17g, sat fat 6g, fibre 8g, sugar 24g, salt 0.39g

Braised beef with onions & mushrooms

Rich, sticky, dark and packed with flavour, this is the kind of dish that puts a smile on everyone's face, even on the bleakest winter day.

TAKES 3–3½ HOURS ● SERVES 6–8

1.5kg/3lb 5oz braising steak, thickly
   sliced
15g/½oz dried porcini mushrooms
3 tbsp olive oil
500g/1lb 2oz red onions (about 3),
   thinly sliced
1 tbsp plain flour
425ml/¾ pint port
250g/9oz chestnut mushrooms, whole,
   or halved if large

1 Heat oven to 160C/140C fan/gas 3. Pat the beef dry with kitchen paper and season. Pour 600ml/1 pint boiling water over the dried mushrooms and leave to soak for 30 minutes. Drain, reserving the juice.

2 Heat 2 tablespoons of the oil in a large flameproof casserole, then fry the meat until browned. Remove the meat, pour in the remaining oil, then fry the onions for 10 minutes until lightly browned. Return the meat to the pan, sprinkle in the flour and cook for 1 minute.

3 Add the port, strained mushroom juices and the soaked mushrooms. Bring to the boil, season, then cover tightly and cook in the oven for 1½–2 hours until the meat is tender. Check after 1 hour and give it a stir, adding a little boiling water if it looks too thick.

4 Add more seasoning, if necessary, then add the chestnut mushrooms and cook for a further 10 minutes.

PER SERVING 570 kcals, protein 54g, carbs 17g, fat 28g, sat fat 10g, fibre 2g, sugar 13g, salt 0.4g

Lamb with lemon & dill

This tasty stew can be made up to 3 days ahead and reheats wonderfully well, plus you can double or even treble the quantities for larger numbers. It freezes well too.

TAKES 1¼ HOURS • SERVES 2

350g/12oz diced lamb
2 tsp plain flour
1 tbsp sunflower oil
1 onion, chopped
300ml/½ pint hot chicken or vegetable stock (a cube or powder is fine)
3 tbsp chopped fresh dill
1 bay leaf
300g/10oz salad potatoes, thickly sliced
zest and juice of ½ lemon
2 tbsp crème fraîche (half-fat is fine)
crusty bread, to serve

1 Toss the lamb in the flour with a little salt and plenty of black pepper. Heat the oil in a heavy-based pan and fry the onion for 5 minutes until softened. Add the lamb and cook, stirring well, until tinged brown.

2 Stir in the stock, 2 tablespoons of the dill and the bay leaf. Bring to the boil then simmer for 30 minutes.

3 Add the potatoes and lemon juice, and cook for a further 30 minutes until the potatoes are tender. Serve in soup plates or individual dishes with a spoonful of crème fraîche and a scattering of lemon zest and the rest of the dill on each serving. Some crusty bread on the side will be good for mopping up all the juices.

PER SERVING 531 kcals, protein 41g, carbs 34g, fat 27g, sat fat 11g, fibre 3g, sugar none, salt 0.86g

Moroccan-style chicken with lentils

This rich chicken dish gets top marks from the children. Serve with rice or couscous and a generous dollop of yogurt.

TAKES 2 HOURS • SERVES 4

2 tbsp olive oil
8 boneless skinless chicken thighs
2 garlic cloves, crushed
1 tbsp ground cumin
1 tbsp ground coriander seeds
1 tbsp sweet paprika
1 large onion, finely sliced
50g/2oz red split lentils
400g can chopped tomatoes
1 tbsp tomato ketchup
700ml/1¼ pints chicken stock
1 cinnamon stick
200g/8oz whole dried apricots
handful of fresh mint leaves, to garnish

1 Heat oven to 180C/160C fan/gas 4. Rub 1 tablespoon of the olive oil into the chicken thighs. Mix the garlic, cumin, coriander and paprika together, then rub all over the chicken thighs on both sides.

2 Heat a large flameproof casserole, add the chicken thighs and cook over a medium heat for 5 minutes until golden on both sides. (You might need to do this in two batches.) Remove the chicken and set aside. Turn down the heat, add the remaining oil and fry the onion for 5 minutes until softened.

3 Stir in the rest of the ingredients, and bring to the boil. Put the chicken thighs on top and pour in any juices. Cover and cook for 1½ hours, until the meat is tender and the sauce thickened. Scatter with the mint leaves and serve.

PER SERVING 461 kcals, protein 48g, carbs 40g, fat 13g, sat fat 3g, fibre 6g, sugar 1g, salt 1.45g

Rabbit & mushroom hotpot

This recipe is based on Lancashire hotpot, in which the meat is layered with sliced potatoes, onions and mushrooms, then cooked in stock.

TAKES 2¼ HOURS ● SERVES 4

3 tbsp olive oil, plus extra for brushing
1 oven-ready rabbit, cut into legs, shoulders and 2 loins (discard the ribcage as it's very bony)
250g pack small flat mushrooms (portabellini), thickly sliced
1kg/2lb 4oz large potatoes, thinly sliced
3 Spanish onions, halved and thinly sliced
1 tbsp chopped fresh rosemary
600ml/1 pint strong-flavoured chicken stock
Savoy cabbage, to serve

1 Heat oven to 180C/160C fan/gas 4. Heat the oil in a deep, flameproof casserole dish, add the rabbit pieces and fry them briefly until browned. Lift the rabbit from the dish on to a plate, add the mushrooms to the dish and quickly stir-fry. Remove the mushrooms to a plate and turn off the heat.
2 Layer half the potatoes in the dish then, seasoning with salt and black pepper as you layer, top with half the onions, mushrooms and rosemary, then top with the rabbit. Now follow with the rest of the onions, mushrooms, rosemary and a neat layer of potatoes. Pour over the stock and brush the potatoes with oil.
3 Put back on the heat and bring to the boil, then cover and put in the oven for 1¼ hours. Remove the lid then return to the oven at 220C/200C fan/gas 7 for 30 minutes more to brown the top. Serve with Savoy cabbage.

PER SERVING 544 kcals, protein 42g, carbs 58g, fat 18g, sat fat 4g, fibre 7g, sugar 11g, salt 1.04g

Asian aubergine & pork hotpot

The slow-cooked aubergines in this casserole become soft and absorb all the flavour of the tender pork and punchy sauce.

TAKES ABOUT 1¾ HOURS

● **SERVES 4**

3 tbsp sunflower oil

750g/1lb 10oz fatty pork, such as shoulder or skinless belly, cut into large chunks

2 aubergines, cut into large chunks

2 tbsp dark muscovado sugar

5 star anise

1 cinnamon stick

2 onions, chopped

very large piece of ginger, peeled and finely sliced

1 red chilli, seeded and sliced

1 bunch coriander, leaves and stalks separated, stalks finely chopped

2 tbsp Thai fish sauce, plus more to taste

juice 1 large lime

1 Heat oven to 200C/180C fan/gas 6. Heat 2 tablespoons of the oil in an ovenproof sauté pan and brown the meat well, then scoop out of the pan. Add the rest of the oil and brown the aubergines, then scoop them out and add to the pork.

2 Tip the sugar into the pan and caramelise it slightly, then return the pork and aubergine to the pan with the star anise and cinnamon, and coat them in the sticky caramel.

3 Add the onions, ginger and half the chilli, and cook for a few minutes. Add the coriander stalks, fish sauce and enough water to come about a third of the way up. Cover and cook in the oven for 1 hour, then remove and add the lime juice and more fish sauce to taste. Stir through half the coriander leaves and the remaining chilli, and scatter over the rest of the coriander leaves.

PER SERVING 574 kcals, protein 38g, carbs 18g, fat 40g, sat fat 13g, fibre 4g, sugar 15g, salt 1.81g

Lamb printanière

Printanière means 'of spring', and this dish is full of the fresh flavours of broad beans, peas and new potatoes. It can be cooked up to the end of step 2 a day in advance.

TAKES ABOUT 3¼ HOURS
- **SERVES 4–6**

1kg/2lb 4oz boned shoulder of lamb
4 shallots, quartered
butter and olive oil, for frying
1 bouquet garni
600ml/1 pint stock
300ml/½ pint white wine
500g/1lb 2oz tiny new potatoes
4 carrots, cut into sticks
500g/1lb 2oz broad beans, podded
500g/1lb 2oz fresh peas, podded
3–4 tbsp crème fraîche
fresh chervil or parsley, to garnish

1 Cut the lamb into large chunks. Fry the shallots gently in a large frying pan in a little butter and oil until softened, but not browned. Remove with a slotted spoon. Fry the lamb until browned – you may need to do this in batches.

2 Add the bouquet garni, shallots, stock and wine to the lamb, and season with salt and black pepper. Bring to the boil, reduce to a gentle simmer, then cover tightly and cook for 1½ hours. Add the potatoes and carrots, and cook for a further 30 minutes.

3 Fish out the bouquet garni and add the beans and peas. Cook for 10 minutes, then season well and stir in the crème fraîche. Ladle into soup bowls and scatter over some chervil or parsley to serve.

PER SERVING (4) 1,019 kcals, protein 65g, carbs 54g, fat 59g, sat fat 29g, fibre 17g, sugar 16g, salt 1.32g

Daube of pork

You can't find a cheaper cut of pork than shoulder and, like most cheap cuts of meat, it's perfectly suited to being slow cooked and comes out irresistibly unctuous.

TAKES 3½ HOURS, PLUS MARINATING

● **SERVES 6–8**

3 tbsp sunflower oil

3kg/6lb 8oz skinned, boned and rolled
    pork shoulder

350ml/12fl oz beef stock

FOR THE MARINADE

75cl bottle full-bodied red wine

300ml/½ pint olive oil

4 plum tomatoes, halved

6 garlic cloves, crushed

2 carrots, sliced

4 celery sticks, sliced

1 leek, trimmed and sliced

1 tsp cumin seeds

1 tsp fennel seeds

½ bunch fresh mint, chopped

3 fresh thyme sprigs

2 bay leaves

1 Combine all the marinade ingredients in a large casserole dish. Heat the sunflower oil in a large heavy-based frying pan until practically smoking, then fry the pork until dark brown all over. Add the pork to the combined marinade ingredients and marinate in the fridge for 24 hours.

2 The next day, heat oven to 180C/160C fan/gas 4. Remove the pork from the marinade and set aside. Tip the marinade into a pan set over a high heat and bring to the boil. Boil for 15 minutes, skimming off any foam from the surface. Add the stock and bring back to the boil, then add the meat. Cover tightly and cook in the oven for 3 hours, turning the meat halfway through.

3 Lift out the pork and keep warm. Strain the cooking liquid into a clean pan. Bring to the boil, then boil to reduce for about 15–20 minutes. Serve the pork with the gravy.

PER SERVING 886 kcals, protein 80g, carbs 13g, fat 58g, sat fat 11g, fibre 2g, sugar 13g, salt 0.87

Beef & stout stew with carrots

This rustic beef stew is packed with sweet, slow-cooked melty carrots. Serve with creamy parsnip mash to complete the meal.

TAKES 3½ HOURS • SERVES 4

2 tbsp vegetable oil
1kg/2lb 4oz stewing beef, cut into large chunks
1 onion, roughly chopped
10 carrots, cut into large chunks
2 tbsp plain flour
500ml can Guinness
1 beef stock cube
pinch of sugar
3 bay leaves
1 large fresh thyme sprig
creamy parsnip mash, to serve

1 Heat oven to 160C/140C fan/gas 3. Heat the oil in a large flameproof casserole dish and brown the meat really well in batches. Set aside. Add the onion and carrots to the dish, give them a good browning, then scatter over the flour and stir.

2 Tip the meat and any juices back into the dish and give it all a good stir. Pour over the Guinness and crumble in the stock cube. Season the stew with salt, black pepper and a pinch of sugar. Tuck in the herbs and bring everything to a simmer.

3 Cover with a lid and put in the oven for about 2½ hours until the meat is really tender. Leave the stew to settle a little before serving with spoonfuls of parsnip mash.

PER SERVING 562 kcals, protein 58g, carbs 26g, fat 23g, sat fat 8g, fibre 6g, sugar 20g, salt 1.5g

Lamb, black pudding & mustard hotpot

This is a twist on the original slow-cooked recipe, but if you're a traditionalist you can simply leave out the black pudding.

TAKES 2¾–3 HOURS • SERVES 4

2 tbsp groundnut or sunflower oil (or dripping)
2 large onions, thinly sliced
350g/12oz black pudding, thickly sliced
8 lamb chops (middle neck cutlets), excess fat trimmed
900g/2lb potatoes, peeled and very thinly sliced
3 carrots, thinly sliced
2 tbsp grainy mustard
20g pack fresh parsley, finely chopped
6 fresh thyme sprigs, leaves only
700ml/1¼ pints hot lamb or beef stock
knob of butter, melted

1 Heat oven to 180C/160C fan/gas 4. Heat half the oil in a frying pan and cook the onions for 5 minutes until starting to turn golden. Remove and set aside. Pour the remaining oil into the pan and fry the black pudding for 1 minute on each side. Remove, drain on kitchen paper and then set aside.

2 Cook the chops in the pan over a high heat until well coloured but not cooked. Set aside.

3 Layer the ingredients in the bottom of a deep casserole dish, starting with some potatoes and carrots, and dotting half the mustard over each layer of black pudding. As you build up the layers, season and sprinkle with the herbs. Top with a layer of overlapping potato slices.

4 Pour over the stock, then brush the top with the butter. Cover and bake for 2 hours, removing the lid for the last half hour to crisp up the potatoes.

PER SERVING 832 kcals, protein 50g, carbs 66g, fat 43g, sat fat 10g, fibre 7g, sugar none, salt 3.1g

Braised chicken chasseur

A bowl of mashed potatoes and some buttered spinach make the perfect partners for this classic. Or just serve with crusty bread to mop up the sauce.

TAKES 1¾ HOURS • SERVES 4

4 chicken legs
2 tbsp olive oil
2 onions, thickly sliced
250g/9oz whole button or chestnut mushrooms
1 rounded tbsp tomato purée
300ml/½ pint white wine
400g can chicken or beef consommé (or use 400ml/14fl oz shop-bought fresh stock, or a cube)
3–4 tomatoes, quartered and seeded
sprinkling of fresh tarragon leaves and chopped parsley, to garnish

1 Season the chicken with salt and black pepper. Heat the oil in a lidded sauté pan or shallow casserole. Pan-fry the chicken over a medium–high heat until golden all over. Remove from the pan and keep to one side.

2 Drain off the fat, leaving around 2 tablespoons in the pan. Add the onions and mushrooms to the pan, and cook for 6–8 minutes, stirring occasionally, until they have a little colour and are just beginning to soften. Stir in the tomato purée and white wine, then pour in the consommé or stock.

3 Return the chicken to the pan and bring to a simmer. Cover and continue to cook, allowing the sauce to just simmer for about 1 hour, or until the meat feels tender when pressed.

4 To finish, skim the sauce of any excess fat then add the tomatoes. Simmer, without the lid, for a further 2–3 minutes to soften them, then scatter over the herbs.

PER SERVING 353 kcals, protein 30g, carbs 20g, fat 22g, sat fat 6g, fibre 2g, sugar 8g, salt 1.69g

Lancashire hotpot

This famous lamb stew topped with sliced potatoes is a leave-to-cook favourite that's simplicity itself to make.

TAKES 2 HOURS • SERVES 4

100g/4oz dripping or butter
900g/2lb stewing lamb, cut into large
   chunks
3 lamb kidneys, sliced, fat removed
2 medium onions, chopped
4 carrots, peeled and sliced
25g/1oz plain flour
2 tsp Worcestershire sauce
500ml/18fl oz lamb or chicken stock
2 bay leaves
900g/2lb potatoes, peeled and sliced

1 Heat oven to 160C/140C fan/gas 3. Heat some of the dripping or butter in a large, shallow casserole dish, brown the lamb in batches, lift on to a plate, then repeat with the kidneys.

2 Fry the onions and carrots in the pan with a little more dripping or butter until golden. Sprinkle over the flour, allow to cook for a couple of minutes, shake over the Worcestershire sauce, pour in the stock, then bring to the boil. Stir in the meat and bay leaves, then turn off the heat. Arrange the sliced potatoes on top of the meat, then dot with a little more dripping or butter. Cover, then put in the oven for about 1½ hours until the potatoes are cooked.

3 Remove the lid, dot the potatoes with more dripping or butter, then turn the oven up to brown the potatoes, or finish under the grill for 5–8 minutes until they are nicely brown.

PER SERVING 993 kcals, protein 70g, carbs 56g, fat 56g, sat fat 26g, fibre 7g, sugar 12g, salt 1.43g

Slow-cooked pork & red cabbage

If you don't want to slice the pork yourself, ask the butcher to do it for you. Either way, don't use ready-sliced as it will be too thin and cook too quickly.

TAKES 2½–2¾ HOURS ● SERVES 6

1.5kg/3lb 5oz pork shoulder
1 rounded tsp black peppercorns, coarsely crushed
1 tbsp fresh thyme leaves
3 tbsp olive oil
2 onions, chopped
1kg/2lb 4oz red cabbage, finely shredded
2 apples, peeled, cored and cut into eighths
425ml/¾ pint red wine
200g pack vacuum-packed chestnuts
2 tbsp cranberry or redcurrant jelly

1 Heat oven to 160C/140C fan/gas 3. Cut the pork into slices about 3cm thick. Sprinkle the peppercorns and thyme over the pork.

2 Heat 2 tablespoons of the oil in a large flameproof casserole, then fry the onions until lightly browned. Stir in the cabbage, add the apples and wine, and cook until the cabbage starts to soften. Add the chestnuts, 1 tablespoon of the jelly and some salt and black pepper, and bring to the boil. Cover and simmer for around 5 minutes.

3 Meanwhile, heat the remaining oil in a frying pan, fry the pork on both sides until browned, then stir in the remaining jelly. Cook for a few minutes until the pork is deeply browned.

4 Arrange the pork in the dish over the cabbage. Pour a little boiling water into the frying pan, stir well, then pour the liquid over the pork. Cover the dish tightly, then cook in the oven for 1¼–1½ hours until the pork is very tender.

PER SERVING 770 kcals, protein 49g, carbs 33g, fat 48g, sat fat 17g, fibre 7g, sugar 21g, salt 0.48g

Braised beef with cinnamon & chilli

Braising beef makes it deliciously tender. The addition of chopped dark chocolate creates a wonderfully rich sauce for this casserole.

TAKES 2 HOURS • SERVES 6

4 tbsp olive oil
140g/5oz diced pancetta
2 onions, roughly chopped
2 garlic cloves, crushed
2 red chillies, seeded and finely sliced
1kg/2lb 4oz braising steak, diced
2 tbsp plain flour
600ml/1 pint beef stock
400g can chopped tomatoes
1 tsp hot chilli powder
1 tsp sugar
1 large cinnamon stick
50g/2oz good-quality dark chocolate, chopped
mashed potatoes or plain boiled rice, to serve

1 Heat oven to 160C/140C fan/gas 3. Heat 1 tablespoon of the oil in a frying pan and cook the pancetta and onions until tender and the pancetta has begun to crisp. Add the garlic and chillies, cook for 1 minute, then, using a slotted spoon, transfer to a casserole dish.

2 Put the beef in a bowl, add the flour, season, then toss to coat, brushing off any excess. Heat another tablespoon of the oil in the frying pan and brown half of the beef, then add to the casserole. Repeat with the remaining beef.

3 Deglaze the pan with the stock and add to the casserole with the tomatoes, chilli, sugar and cinnamon. Bring to the boil, cover tightly, then braise in the oven for 1½ hours or until the meat is tender. Remove from the oven, then add the chocolate, stirring until melted and thoroughly combined. Season and serve with mashed potatoes or rice.

PER SERVING 762 kcals, protein 64g, carbs 22g, fat 47g, sat fat 17g, fibre 3g, sugar 5g, salt 3g

Lemon & garlic turkey roast

Turkey is a good-value meat and healthy, too, as it's low in fat and the dark meat is high in zinc and vitamin B. Drumsticks make a low-cost Sunday lunch.

TAKES 1 HOUR 50 MINUTES

● **SERVES 6**

3 lemons
100g/4oz butter, softened
1 tsp dried sage
3 garlic cloves, crushed
2 large turkey drumsticks
2 large onions, roughly chopped
200g/8oz long grain rice
600ml/1 pint hot vegetable stock

1 Heat oven to 190C/170C fan/gas 5. Finely grate the zest of two of the lemons and set aside, then squeeze the juice of one of these lemons. Thinly slice the remaining lemon. Mash together the butter, lemon zest, sage and garlic. Season. Loosen the turkey skin and spread a quarter of the flavoured butter under the skin of each drumstick. Arrange the lemon slices on top of the butter. Put on a baking sheet, cover with foil and roast for 30 minutes.

2 Meanwhile, melt the remaining flavoured butter in a roasting tin on the hob. Cook the onions for 8 minutes until soft. Stir in the rice, stock and lemon juice and bring to the boil.

3 Transfer the turkey to a wire rack and put it on top of the rice. Bake, uncovered, for 30–35 minutes. Fluff up the rice with a fork. Season. Carve the turkey and serve with the rice.

PER SERVING 484 kcals, protein 34g, carbs 35g, fat 24g, sat fat 12g, fibre 1g, sugar none, salt 0.95g

Peppered duck with red wine gravy

Marinating the fruit in crème de cassis gives this surprisingly ungreasy duck dish a rich colour and a delicious blackcurranty flavour.

TAKES 2¼ HOURS • SERVES 4

100g/4oz each fresh blackcurrants and redcurrants (or frozen and thawed)

3 tbsp crème de cassis

1 whole duck (about 2.25–2.7kg/5–6lb)

1 tbsp mixed peppercorns, coarsely crushed

1 tbsp plain flour

300ml/½ pint red wine

200ml/7fl oz fresh chicken stock

1 Put the fruit and cassis in a bowl and set aside while you cook the duck.

2 Heat oven to 220C/200C fan/gas 7. Weigh the duck, prick the skin with a fork, then season with the peppercorns and some salt. Put in a roasting tin. Roast the duck for about 15 minutes until it starts to sizzle. Reduce the heat to 180C/160C fan/gas 4 and roast for a further 20 minutes per 450g/1lb. Transfer the duck to a plate, cover with foil and leave to rest for 15 minutes.

3 Pour off all but a tablespoon of fat from the tin and put the tin on the hob. Stir in the flour and cook, stirring, until well browned. Add the wine and stock, and cook, stirring, until glossy and thickened slightly. Add the cassis and fruit mixture, and simmer gently for 6–8 minutes until the fruit is softened. Carve the duck and serve with the gravy.

PER SERVING 927 kcals, protein 40g, carbs 11g, fat 74g, sat fat 20g, fibre 2g, sugar none, salt 0.61g.

Rack of lamb with an apricot & mustard crust

Rack of lamb is an expensive cut, but it's worth it as there is little waste and it looks and tastes great filled with a fruity stuffing.

TAKES 2 HOURS • SERVES 6

140g/5oz fresh white breadcrumbs
4 tbsp chopped fresh parsley
1 tbsp chopped fresh rosemary
1 tsp grated lemon zest
8 ready-to-eat dried apricots, roughly
    chopped
2 tbsp olive oil
1 small egg, beaten
1 tbsp Dijon mustard
2 French-trimmed and chined racks of
    lamb, each with 8 chops (about
    1.25kg/2lb 12oz total) (ask your
    butcher to leave the surrounding fat
    on so the racks are joined)
2 garlic cloves, chopped

FOR THE RED WINE SAUCE

300ml/½ pint red wine
300ml/½ pint hot lamb stock
2 tsp Dijon mustard
1–2 tbsp apricot jam
knob of butter, chilled

1 Heat oven to 220C/200C fan/gas 7. Mix together the breadcrumbs, parsley, rosemary, lemon zest, apricots, oil and egg. Spread half the mustard over the inside curves of the lamb, sprinkle with garlic and season.

2 Spoon half the crumb mixture on top of one rack, then press the other rack on top, enclosing the filling and crossing the bones. Tie with string, spread the remaining mustard on the outside of the racks and firmly press on the remaining crumb mixture.

3 Roast in a tin for 10 minutes then lower heat to 190C/170C fan/gas 5 and cook for a further 50 minutes–1 hour. Transfer the lamb to a plate and keep warm.

4 Put the roasting tin on the heat, add the wine and bubble rapidly for 3–4 minutes until reduced to a syrup. Add the stock, then stir in the mustard and jam, and cook for a few minutes. Whisk in the butter and season. Remove the string, slice the lamb and serve with the sauce.

PER SERVING 484 kcals, protein 38g, carbs 27g, fat 22g, sat fat 9g, fibre 2g, sugar 2g, salt 1.25g

Chicken with wild mushroom sauce

Choose a free-range chicken for a better taste and texture. The Drambuie adds a wonderful flavour to the creamy herb sauce.

TAKES 2½ HOURS • SERVES 6

1 chicken (about 2.25kg/5lb), preferably free-range

knob of softened butter

bouquet garni of fresh tarragon, parsley and bay leaves

FOR THE MUSHROOM SAUCE

300g/10oz mixed mushrooms, sliced or quartered

100ml/3½fl oz Drambuie

425ml/¾ pint fresh chicken stock

142ml pot double cream

3 tbsp roughly chopped fresh tarragon

1 Heat oven to 190C/170C fan/gas 5. Put the chicken in a roasting tin and rub it with the butter. Season generously. Tie the herbs together and put them in the cavity of the bird.

2 Roast the chicken, allowing around 20 minutes per 450g/1lb, plus an extra 20 minutes. Transfer the chicken to a warm plate and cover loosely with foil.

3 Pour off all but 1 tablespoon of fat from the tin and put the tin on the hob, then fry the mushrooms for 1–2 minutes until lightly browned. Keeping the heat quite high, deglaze the pan with the Drambuie for 1–2 minutes, scraping the base of the pan with a wooden spoon. Add the stock and bubble until reduced by half. Stir in the cream and bring just to the boil. Stir in the tarragon and season. Carve the chicken and serve with the sauce poured over.

PER SERVING 528 kcals, protein 43g, carbs 5g, fat 33g, sat fat 15g, fibre trace, sugar none, salt 0.67g

Sticky belly pork

Cheap cuts, like these belly strips, are good for barbecuing. By slow roasting the meat first, then crisping it up quickly on the barbecue to finish, the meat stays really tender.

TAKES 4½ HOURS • SERVES 8

1.6kg/3lb 8oz pork belly
3 tbsp light muscovado sugar
3 tbsp treacle
3 tbsp tomato purée
1 onion, whizzed in a food processor
3 garlic cloves, crushed
1 tbsp dried oregano
1 tbsp ground cumin
1 tsp crushed dried chillies
1 tsp ground cinnamon

1 Heat oven to 150C/130C fan/gas 2, then sit the pork belly in a deep roasting tin. Mix the remaining ingredients with 1 teaspoon salt, then rub all over the pork. Cover, roast for 3 hours, then uncover, slice the pork into 16 short fat chops. Spoon over the sauce from the tin, then roast, uncovered, for another hour, turning the strips halfway through cooking. Cool, cover, then chill for up to 24 hours.

2 About 15 minutes before you are ready to barbecue, pop the pork into a low oven to melt the sauce, making sure the strips are nicely coated in it. Barbecue skin-side down first to crisp up, then cook for just a few minutes, turning, until heated through and the sauce is sticky.

PER SERVING 427 kcals, protein 34g, carbs 10g, fat 28g, sat fat 11g, fibre none, sugar 8g, salt 0.82g

Guinea fowl with mustard & lemon roots

If you love chicken but would like a bit more flavour, this is the bird for you. It has a firm texture and a slightly gamey flavour, without being too strong.

TAKES 1¾ HOURS • SERVES 4

1 guinea fowl (about 1.5kg/3lb 5oz)

1 lemon

2 tbsp grainy mustard

3 tbsp olive oil

3–4 large leeks

3–4 large carrots, peeled and cut into chunks

750g/1lb 10oz floury potatoes, peeled and cut into chunks

300ml/½ pint white wine

8 thin-sliced rashers streaky bacon

1 Heat oven to 180C/160C fan/gas 4. Wipe the guinea fowl and season all over with salt and black pepper, then put in a large roasting tin. Finely grate the zest of the lemon and scrape it into a large bowl. Add the mustard and oil and mix well. Halve the lemon and put the pieces inside the bird. Roast the guinea fowl for 30 minutes.

2 Meanwhile, cut each leek into 3–4 chunks. Add all the veggies to the oil and mustard, and mix until well coated.

3 When the guinea fowl has been roasting for 30 minutes, add the veggies around the bird, sprinkle with a little salt and return to the oven for a further 45 minutes. Splash the wine around the bird and over the veggies, and lay the bacon over the guinea fowl. Return to the oven for 15–20 minutes, until the bacon is crisp and brown, and the veggies are tender.

PER SERVING 863 kcals, protein 80g, carbs 43g, fat 35g, sat fat 10g, fibre 7g, sugar none, salt 1.88g

Roasted sirloin with red onions & port gravy

Sirloin is an expensive cut of beef but will reward you with tender, succulent slices. It looks splendid with its herb coating, surrounded by roasted red onions.

TAKES 1¾ HOURS • SERVES 6–8

1.3kg/3lb boneless beef sirloin joint
4 red onions
2 tbsp olive oil
4 tbsp chopped fresh parsley
1 tbsp chopped fresh thyme
1 tbsp chopped fresh rosemary
2 tbsp horseradish sauce

FOR THE GRAVY

1 tbsp plain flour
150ml/¼ pint port
300ml/½ pint beef stock
1 tsp Worcestershire sauce

1 Season the meat with salt and black pepper. Quarter the onions through the root, keeping the root intact. Peel the onion quarters.

2 Heat the oil in a roasting tin and add the onions, turning them until they are glistening. Put the beef in the tin and surround with the onions. Mix the herbs together in a bowl.

3 Heat oven to 180C/160C fan/gas 4. Roast the meat for 1¼–1½ hours for medium. Halfway through cooking, spread the horseradish over the fat of the meat and sprinkle over three-quarters of the mixed herbs.

4 Transfer the meat and onions to a warm serving platter and cover with foil. Reheat the pan juices in the tin on the hob, stir in the flour and cook for 1 minute. Stir in the port, then the stock. Bring to the boil, stirring until thickened. Add the Worcestershire sauce and remaining mixed herbs. Simmer for 5 minutes. Serve with the carved meat.

PER SERVING (6) 468 kcals, protein 51g, carbs 12g, fat 23g, sat fat 9g, fibre 1g, sugar 8g, salt 0.64g

Slow-roasted Greek-style lamb

Once you've prepared this simple dish, you can relax and pour yourself a glass of wine while the lamb simmers away slowly in the oven.

TAKES 2 HOURS • SERVES 1

2 tbsp olive oil
1 lamb shank (about 400g/14oz)
1 small red onion, peeled, halved and
thickly sliced
1 medium potato, peeled and
quartered
4 garlic cloves, peeled and left whole
4 fresh rosemary sprigs
1 tbsp tomato purée
230g can chopped tomatoes
125ml/4fl oz white wine
crusty bread, to serve

1 Heat the oil in a small casserole dish. Season the lamb shank with salt and black pepper, and fry in the hot oil for 10 minutes, turning often to brown it all over. Remove from the dish and set aside.

2 Heat oven to 180C/160C fan/gas 4. Fry the onion slices in the same oil as the lamb for about 8 minutes until they start to colour, then stir in the potato, garlic and rosemary, and continue to cook for another 2 minutes so that everything is coated in the oil.

3 Stir in the tomato purée, tomatoes and white wine, season and bring to a simmer. Nestle the lamb shank in the mixture, cover, and put in the oven. Cook for 1½ hours or until the lamb is very tender, turning once halfway through cooking. Serve with some crusty bread.

PER SERVING 538 kcals, protein 34g, carbs 19g, fat 34g, sat fat 12g, fibre 3g, sugar none, salt 0.52g

Catalan chicken with white wine juices

Roasting with wine in the tin makes the chicken really moist and a brush of spice paste enlivens the traditional roast.

TAKES ABOUT 1¾ HOURS • SERVES 4

1 chicken (about 1.8kg/4lb), preferably free-range
300ml/½ pint dry white wine, e.g. Rioja
fresh bay leaves, to garnish

FOR THE SPICE PASTE

5 tbsp clear honey
juice of 1 lemon
1½ tsp ground cumin
4 garlic cloves, crushed

1 Heat oven to 180C/160C fan/gas 4. Season inside the chicken with salt and black pepper, and put it in a roasting tin. Mix the honey, lemon juice, cumin and garlic for the spice paste together with some seasoning, and brush half over the chicken. Roast the chicken for around 30 minutes, brushing with more spice paste after 15 minutes.

2 Pour the wine round the chicken then return it to the oven for 1 hour, brushing it every so often with the remaining spice paste.

3 When ready, rest the chicken for 10–15 minutes, then garnish with the bay leaves and serve with the roasting juices (minus any fat), with some roast potatoes and spinach on the side.

PER SERVING 481 kcals, protein 37g, carbs 16g, fat 25g, sat fat 8g, fibre none, sugar 14g, salt 0.43g

Salt & pepper turkey

A finishing touch of a lattice of bacon gives centre-stage appeal to this turkey. Serve with classic roasties and your favourite stuffing.

TAKES 4–4½ HOURS • SERVES 8–10 WITH LEFTOVERS

1 tbsp black peppercorns
1 tbsp Maldon sea salt
1 lemon
1 turkey (about 4.5–5.6kg/10–12lb), thawed if frozen, giblets removed
a few bay leaves, plus extra sprigs to garnish
stuffing of your choice (optional)
50g/2oz butter, melted
10–12 rashers streaky bacon

1 Heat oven to 190C/170C fan/gas 5. Coarsely crush the peppercorns and add the salt. Finely grate the lemon over the top and mix in the zest with the seasoning. Quarter the lemon and put it inside the turkey with a few bay leaves.
2 If you are stuffing the turkey, stuff the neck end only and secure the neck flap with a skewer, then tie the legs together. Weigh the turkey and calculate the cooking time at 18 minutes per 450g/1lb.
3 Set the turkey in a roasting tin. Brush all over with butter. Sprinkle the salt and black pepper mix over the breast and legs. Cover loosely with foil and roast for the calculated cooking time, basting every hour. Half an hour before the end of the cooking time, remove the foil. Arrange the bacon in a lattice over the breast and return the turkey to the oven. When the turkey is cooked, transfer it to a platter, cover with foil and rest for 15–30 minutes before carving.

PER SERVING (8) 644 kcals, protein 91g, carbs 9g, fat 25g, sat fat 9g, fibre none, sugar 4g, salt 3.59g

Roast lamb with anchovies, orange & rosemary

Anchovies give a wonderful savouriness to the lamb, which is lifted by the aromas of orange zest and rosemary. The orange juice can be added to a gravy.

TAKES ABOUT 2½ HOURS, PLUS MARINATING AND RESTING
- **SERVES 4–6**

1 leg of lamb (about 2kg/4lb 8oz)
50g can anchovy fillets in oil, drained, halved and oil reserved
small bunch of fresh rosemary, leaves only
zest of 2 oranges
2 tbsp olive oil or the reserved anchovy oil

1 Lay the lamb on a board and, using the tip of a sharp knife, make 12 slits over the meat in a criss-cross pattern. Fill the slits with the anchovy halves and rosemary leaves. Mix together the orange zest, olive or anchovy oils, then rub over the meat. Season with black pepper, then cover and refrigerate for an hour or so to intensify the flavours.

2 Heat oven to 180C/160C fan/gas 4. Put the lamb in a roasting tin and roast for 25 minutes per 450g/1lb for medium, or 30 minutes per 450g/1lb for well done.

3 Remove from the oven, cover with foil and leave to rest in a warm place for 15–20 minutes before carving. Serve with purple sprouting broccoli or spring greens and some rice stirred through with pistachio nuts.

PER SERVING (4) 633 kcals, protein 70g, carbs 1g, fat 39g, sat fat 17g, fibre none, sugar none, salt 1.13g

Spiced honey-roast pork loin

Marinating the pork gives it gutsy flavours and the meat smells amazing while it's slow cooking. Serve with roast potatoes and broccoli.

TAKES 2½ HOURS, PLUS MARINATING
- **SERVES 8**

100ml/3½fl oz olive oil

3 tbsp clear honey

3kg/6lb 8oz boned and rolled loin of pork

1 tbsp ground cumin

1 tbsp dried sage

1 tsp celery salt

FOR THE GRAVY

25g/1oz butter

25g/1oz plain flour

300ml/½ pint dry white wine

600ml/1 pint vegetable stock (a cube is fine)

1 Whisk together the oil and honey, and rub this all over the pork. Combine the dry ingredients on a large plate, then roll the pork in it until it is covered. Leave to marinate for a couple of hours.

2 Heat oven to 180C/160C fan/gas 4. Fit a rack over a large roasting tin. Put the pork on the rack, season and roast for 50 minutes. Reduce the heat to 160C/140C fan/gas 3 and cook the pork for another 1 hour 10 minutes or until cooked through. Cover with foil and rest on a board for 10–20 minutes.

3 Melt the butter for the gravy in a pan over a low heat, then whisk in the flour until smooth. Gradually pour in the wine and cook for 2 minutes. Stir in the stock. Leave to cook for 15 minutes until reduced by about a third, tip in any juices from the resting meat and serve.

PER SERVING 783 kcals, protein 69g, carbs 8g, fat 53g, sat fat 19g, fibre none, sugar 3g, salt 1.02g

Slow-roasted chicken

If your chicken often turns out dry, this simple recipe is for you. Slow roasting the bird ensures it is moist and tender – even the breast.

TAKES 2 HOURS 25 MINUTES, PLUS RESTING • SERVES 4

1 chicken (about 1.8–2.25kg/4–5lb), preferably free-range
50g/2oz butter, softened

1 Heat oven to 200C/180C fan/gas 6. Put the chicken in a roasting tin and smear with the butter. Season well and roast for 20 minutes. Turn the heat down to 160C/140C fan/gas 3, add a splash of water to the tin, cover with foil and continue roasting for 1 hour, then remove the foil.

2 Baste the chicken and cook for 50 minutes more. To check the bird is cooked through, insert a skewer or the point of a sharp knife into the thigh (don't hit the bone). When the juices run clear, the bird is cooked. Remove the chicken from the oven, cover with foil and leave to rest for about 20 minutes before carving. Serve with the traditional roast accompaniments, or with spicy couscous for a change.

PER SERVING 563 kcals, protein 57g, carbs 1g, fat 37g, sat fat 15g, fibre none, sugar 1g, salt 0.66g

Rare beef with mustard Yorkshires

*Rib of beef has to be one of the classics. We used a large 2-bone rib for this recipe.
Serve with horseradish, gravy and your favourite veg.*

TAKES ABOUT 3¼–3¾ HOURS

● **SERVES 8**

4 garlic cloves
2 tbsp fresh lemon thyme leaves
1 tbsp black peppercorns
1 tbsp wholegrain mustard
4 anchovy fillets
2 tbsp olive oil
2.7kg/6lb rib of beef, French-trimmed
    and at room temperature
12–16 potatoes, peeled and halved or
    quartered
4 tbsp sunflower oil

FOR THE YORKSHIRES

175ml/6fl oz full-fat milk
2 eggs and 1 egg white
1 tbsp wholegrain mustard
100g/4oz plain flour
8 tbsp sunflower oil

1 Heat oven to 220C/200C fan/gas 7. Grind the garlic, thyme, peppercorns, mustard, anchovies and olive oil in a pestle and mortar. Rub the paste over the beef and put in a roasting tin. Roast for 25 minutes, then turn down the oven to 160C/140C fan/gas 3.

2 Remove the tin from the oven, add the potatoes and toss them in the fat, adding the sunflower oil. Return to the oven for 90 minutes for rare; 2 hours for medium–rare.

3 Make the milk up to 200ml/8fl oz with water. Beat the eggs, egg white, mustard and milk together, then gradually add the flour and a pinch of salt. Pour the batter into a jug. Take the meat out of the oven, cover, and leave to rest, then turn the oven up to 220C/200C fan/gas 7.

4 Put 1 tablespoon oil each in 8 Yorkshire pudding tins and heat in the oven with the potatoes for 15 minutes, on a lower shelf. Pour the batter into the tins; cook for 15–20 minutes until risen.

PER SERVING 767 kcals, protein 60g, carbs 41g, fat 41g, sat fat 14g, fibre 3g, sugar 2g, salt 0.75g

Prepare-ahead turkey roll

Whole turkey breasts are available from larger supermarkets, or order them from your butcher. This makes an easy-carve turkey roast.

TAKES 1¾ HOURS • SERVES 6

4 fresh bay leaves
4 garlic cloves
20g pack dried porcini mushrooms
100ml/3½fl oz dry sherry (fino) or dry
   white wine
7 rashers bacon
2 large skinless turkey breasts (about
   900g/2lb)
400ml/14fl oz chicken stock
1 tbsp soy sauce

1 Heat oven to 200C/180C fan/gas 6. Roughly chop the bay leaves, garlic and mushrooms, and tip into a bowl with a pinch of salt. Pour over the sherry or wine and stir.

2 Lay the bacon rashers on a large piece of buttered foil. Put a turkey breast on top (the bacon should cover it). Spoon over the garlic mix and sandwich with the other turkey breast. Season well and wrap up tightly like a cracker (the turkey roll can be chilled for 24 hours).

3 Roast for 1½ hours until cooked. Leave to rest for 10 minutes before carving. Boil the stock with the soy sauce and the juices from the turkey, and serve as a gravy alongside the sliced turkey.

PER SERVING 266 kcals, protein 44g, carbs 2g, fat 8g, sat fat 3g, fibre 1g, sugar 1g, salt 1.59g

Roast pork with jerk spices

Ring the changes on a Sunday with this Jamaican-style roast. Allspice is so called as it smells of a mixture of cloves, nutmeg and cinnamon.

TAKES 2½–2¾ HOURS, PLUS MARINATING • SERVES 6

FOR THE SPICE PASTE

6 spring onions, roughly chopped

3 garlic cloves

1 tsp ground allspice

1 tsp dried chilli flakes

½ tsp ground ginger

2 tsp fresh or 1 tsp dried thyme leaves

2 tbsp sunflower oil

2 tbsp dark rum

juice of 1 lime

FOR THE PORK AND POTATOES

2kg/4lb 8oz prime boneless pork shoulder joint

1kg /2lb 4oz sweet potatoes, peeled and cut into large chunks

2 red onions, cut into large wedges

3 tbsp olive oil

green vegetables (optional), to serve

1 Put all the spice-paste ingredients into a food processor with ½ teaspoon salt and blend together.

2 Slash the rind of the pork as much as you can with a really sharp knife; the more you cut the better the crackling will be. Rub spice paste all over the meat (not the rind) and marinate for at least 1 hour at room temperature or overnight in the fridge.

3 Dry the rind of the pork and rub generously with salt. Heat oven to 190C/170C fan/gas 5 and roast in a large roasting tin for 1 hour 20 minutes.

4 Toss the potatoes with the onions and oil. Scatter round the pork and return to the oven for 40 minutes more until the potatoes are tender. Lift the pork on to a platter and leave to rest for 10 minutes before carving. Serve with the potatoes and pan juices (skimmed of fat) and some green vegetables, if you like.

PER SERVING 805 kcals, protein 61g, carbs 40g, fat 45g, sat fat 15g, fibre 5g, sugar none, salt 0.59g

Mediterranean leg of lamb

Aubergines, potatoes and tomatoes are roasted in and around a leg of lamb, soaking up all the lovely Mediterranean flavours from the wine, garlic and herbs.

TAKES 1 HOUR 40 MINUTES, PLUS MARINATING • SERVES 6

2 tsp coriander seeds
4 tsp fresh oregano or 1 tsp dried
4 garlic cloves, roughly chopped
150ml/¼ pint white wine
1 leg of lamb (2kg/4lb 8oz)
1kg/2lb 4oz red-skinned potatoes, such as Desiree
500g/1lb 2oz large tomatoes
2 aubergines
2 tbsp olive oil
a few fresh oregano sprigs

1 Crush the coriander, oregano and garlic in a pestle and mortar with some salt and black pepper to form a thick paste. Add a splash of the wine. Make several slits in the lamb and rub with the spice mixture, then set aside for at least 1 hour.

2 Heat oven to 220C/200C fan/gas 7. Cut the potatoes, tomatoes and aubergines into 1cm-thick slices. Put the lamb in a roasting tin, drizzle over the oil and scatter the vegetables around the meat. Pour over the wine, sprinkle with oregano sprigs, season, then roast for 10 minutes. Lower the heat to 180C/160C fan/gas 4 and roast for 1¼ hours until the lamb is cooked.

3 Transfer the lamb to a plate, cover with foil and allow to rest. If necessary, cook the vegetables for another 10 minutes. Carve the lamb and serve with the veg.

PER SERVING 743 kcals, protein 55g, carbs 34g, fat 42g, sat fat 19g, fibre 5g, sugar none, salt 0.43g

Broad bean stuffed onions

You can use ordinary onions for this recipe, but red onions have a slightly sweeter flavour that complements the broad beans perfectly.

TAKES 1 HOUR 10 MINUTES
- **SERVES 4**

4 medium red onions
2 tbsp olive oil
1 garlic clove, finely chopped
100g/4oz broad beans (shelled weight), outer skins removed
100g/4oz firm goat's cheese, diced
2 tbsp chopped basil leaves, plus extra leaves to garnish

1 Heat oven to 190C/170C fan/gas 5. Trim the roots of the onions, but leave the bases intact so that the onions hold together. Slice the top 2.5cm off the tops of the onions and ease out the centres, leaving the shells about three layers thick. Finely chop half of the removed centres, and discard the other half.

2 Heat 1 tablespoon of the oil in a pan and add the chopped onion. Fry for around 3 minutes, until softened, then add the garlic and fry for a further minute. Set aside.

3 Blanch the broad beans in boiling water for 2–3 minutes, then drain well. Mix the goat's cheese and basil with the onion and garlic mixture, and stir in the beans along with plenty of seasoning. Spoon the mixture into the onion shells and transfer to a roasting tin.

4 Brush the onions with the remaining oil and bake for 45 minutes–1 hour until the onions are tender. Serve garnished with the extra basil.

PER SERVING 190 kcals, protein 7g, carbs 10g, fat 14g, sat fat 5g, fibre 3g, sugar none, salt 0.38g

Warm bean cheesecake

*This luscious cheesecake should be eaten warm from the oven, but is delicious cold,
with the remaining beans, basil and tomatoes tossed in a balsamic vinegar dressing.*

TAKES 2 HOURS 10 MINUTES

● **SERVES 8**

100g/4oz butter

125g/4½oz unsweetened bran biscuits,
   finely crushed

50g/2oz mixed sesame and sunflower
   seeds

250g/9oz cream cheese

300ml/½ pint soured cream

4 medium eggs

15g pack basil leaves, torn

150g/5½oz mature Cheddar, grated

500g/1lb 2oz fresh broad beans,
   shelled, or 140g/5oz shelled weight

350g/12oz fine green beans, trimmed

250g/9oz runner beans, thinly sliced

250g/9oz fresh peas, shelled, or
   85g/3oz shelled weight

350g/12oz tomatoes, skinned,
   quartered and seeded, then each
   quarter halved

1 Heat oven to 180C/160C fan/gas 4.
Line the base and sides of a loose-
bottomed 20cm-round cake tin with
baking paper. Melt half the butter, mix
in the biscuits and seeds. Press into the
base of the tin. Chill.

2 Beat together the cream cheese,
soured cream, eggs and some seasoning.
Stir in half the basil and the Cheddar.

3 Boil the broad beans for 3 minutes.
Drain, and plunge them into cold water
to stop the cooking process. Remove the
skins. Boil the green and runner beans
and the peas for 3 minutes. Drain, then
toss with the broad beans. Season and
spoon two-thirds of the mixture into the
tin. Pour over the cheese mixture and
bake for 1–1¼ hours – cover with foil if it
is over browning.

4 Melt the remaining butter in a pan.
Fry the tomatoes and remaining beans
and peas for 3–4 minutes. Toss with the
remaining basil and season. Remove the
cheesecake from the tin and top with
the tomato–bean mixture.

PER SERVING 572 kcals, protein 16g, carbs 18g,
fat 49g, sat fat 27g, fibre 4g, sugar 2g, salt 1.13g

Smoked butternut chilli

We have used smoked paprika in this recipe, which is available in most large supermarkets, but if you can't get hold of it, use ordinary paprika instead.

TAKES 1¼ HOURS • SERVES 6

1 tsp cumin seeds
2 tbsp vegetable oil
1 large onion, finely chopped
1 red chilli, seeded and finely chopped
2 garlic cloves, crushed
2 tsp smoked paprika
1 butternut squash (about 800g/1lb 12oz), cut into chunks
2 orange-fleshed sweet potatoes (about 500g/1lb 2oz), peeled and cut into wedges
2 × 400g cans chopped tomatoes
2 tbsp tomato purée
1 red and 1 yellow pepper, seeded and cut into chunks
420g can mixed pulses
fresh coriander leaves, to garnish

1 Dry-fry the cumin seeds in a wok for 1 minute. Add the oil and stir-fry the onion and chilli for 2–3 minutes. Stir in the garlic, paprika, butternut squash and sweet potatoes, and stir-fry for 2–3 minutes over a high heat. Add the tomatoes, purée, 300ml/½ pint water and season. Bring to the boil, cover and simmer for 20 minutes.

2 Stir in the peppers and bring back to the boil. Simmer, uncovered, for a further 20 minutes. Stir in the pulses and cook for a further 10 minutes. Adjust the seasoning to taste and serve scattered with the fresh coriander leaves.

PER SERVING 305 kcals, protein 11g, carbs 54g, fat 7g, sat fat 1g, fibre 10g, sugar none, salt 0.72g

Bortsch

This recipe for the classic soup is quite chunky; if you prefer a smoother version, simply whizz it in a food processor.

TAKES 2 HOURS • SERVES 6

700g/1lb 9oz raw beetroot, peeled
1 large carrot, peeled
25g/1oz butter
1 onion, very finely chopped
1 celery stick, very finely chopped
2 large tomatoes, skinned, seeded and
 finely chopped
2 garlic cloves, crushed
1.2 litres/2 pints hot vegetable stock
few fresh parsley sprigs
1 bay leaf
2 whole cloves
1–2 tbsp lemon juice

1 Grate the beetroot and carrot. Melt the butter in a large pan and add the beetroot, carrot, onion and celery, and cook over a medium heat for 15 minutes, stirring occasionally until softened but not browned.

2 Add the tomatoes and garlic, and cook for a further 10 minutes until the tomatoes are very soft.

3 Pour in the stock and season with salt and black pepper. Bring to the boil. Package the parsley, bay leaf and cloves together in a piece of muslin tied with string and drop it into the pan. As soon as the soup comes to the boil, cover, reduce the heat and simmer for 1 hour, stirring occasionally. Remove the muslin bag and season with salt, black pepper and the lemon juice. Ladle the soup into bowls and serve.

PER SERVING 155 kcals, protein 4g, carbs 15g, fat 9g, sat fat 5g, fibre 4g, sugar none, salt 1.03g

Pasta with roasted shallots, beetroot & cauliflower

This is an easy dish to make for a midweek dinner and you can roast whatever veg happens to be in season. Blanching the shallots just makes them easier to peel.

TAKES 1¼ HOURS • SERVES 4

4 large raw beetroots
3 tbsp olive oil
16 shallots, blanched, then peeled
1 cauliflower, broken into large pieces
   with the florets intact
350g/12oz penne or rigatoni
250g pack feta
100g bag baby rocket leaves, washed
   and trimmed

1 Heat oven to 200C/180C fan/gas 6. Tip the beetroots into a roasting tin, drizzle over half the olive oil and sprinkle generously with salt and black pepper. Roast for 30 minutes, then add the shallots and cauliflower. Toss everything together and put it back in the oven for a further 35 minutes until the shallots are golden, turning halfway through.

2 Meanwhile, cook the pasta according to the packet instructions. Drain, then set aside.

3 Remove the tin from the oven and transfer the beetroot to a chopping board – discard the skins and tail, which will slip off easily. Roughly chop and return to the tin. Tip in the pasta, crumble over the feta and sprinkle with the rocket. Toss gently to combine, then serve straight away.

PER SERVING 617 kcals, protein 27g, carbs 78g, fat 24g, sat fat 9g, fibre 7g, sugar none, salt 2.47g

Moroccan tagine

This comforting, spicy supper is easily doubled and freezes well, too. It's packed with goodness and contains five of your 5-a-day.

TAKES 2 HOURS ● SERVES 6

FOR THE CHERMOULA PASTE

2 red onions, chopped

3 garlic cloves

small thumb-sized piece of ginger, peeled

100ml/3½fl oz lemon juice (about 3 lemons)

100ml/3½fl oz olive oil

1 tbsp each honey, ground cumin, paprika and turmeric

1 tsp hot chilli powder

handful of fresh coriander, chopped

FOR THE TAGINE

1 tbsp olive oil

3 carrots, cut into chunks

3 large parsnips, cut into chunks

3 red onions, cut into chunks

2 large potatoes, cut into chunks

4 leeks, ends trimmed and cut into chunks

12 dried prunes, dates or figs

2 fresh mint sprigs, leaves only, finely chopped, to garnish

couscous or crusty bread, to serve

1 To make the chermoula, whizz together the paste ingredients in a blender. Heat oven to 220C/200C fan/gas 7.

2 Tip the oil and vegetables for the tagine into a flameproof casserole and cook on the hob for about 7 minutes until lightly browned. You may have to do this in two batches.

3 Add the chermoula paste to the casserole, along with the dried fruit. Pour in 400ml/14fl oz water, cover with a lid and cook in the oven for 45 minutes. Reduce the heat to 180C/160C fan/gas 4 and cook for another 45 minutes. Sprinkle with the mint. Serve on its own or with couscous or crusty bread.

PER SERVING 393 kcals, protein 8g, carbs 52g, fat 18g, sat fat 2g, fibre 10g, sugar 2g, salt 0.12g

Butter bean & squash crumble

This is a really healthy treat – low in fat, high in fibre, a good source of iron, and it counts as four of your 5-a-day.

TAKES 2¾ HOURS • SERVES 6

350g/12oz dried butter beans, soaked overnight in cold water
4 tbsp olive oil
2 onions, chopped
4 garlic cloves, finely chopped
1–2 red chillies, seeded and finely chopped
700g jar passata
1 bouquet garni
425ml/¾ pint white wine
425ml/¾ pint vegetable stock
700g/1lb 9oz squash, peeled, seeded and cut into chunks

FOR THE CRUMBLE

50g/2oz breadcrumbs
25g/1oz walnuts, finely chopped
1 tbsp chopped fresh rosemary
4 tbsp chopped fresh parsley

1 Rinse the beans and put them in a large pan with plenty of water to cover. Bring to the boil, reduce the heat and cook, partly covered, for about 1 hour until tender. Drain well.

2 Heat 2 tablespoons of the oil in a large pan, add the onions and fry for 10 minutes until lightly browned. Add the garlic, chillies, passata, bouquet garni, wine, stock and some salt and black pepper, and bring to the boil. Reduce the heat and simmer, uncovered, for 20 minutes, then add the squash and cook for a further 20 minutes. Taste and add more seasoning, if necessary.

3 Heat oven to 180C/160C fan/gas 4. Stir the beans into the sauce, then transfer to a 2.5-litre gratin dish. Mix together all the crumble ingredients, plus the remaining oil, then sprinkle over the beans. Bake for 30 minutes until the topping is golden and crisp.

PER SERVING 428 kcals, protein 17g, carbs 62g, fat 12g, sat fat 2g, fibre 13g, sugar 18g, salt 0.93g

Pumpkin & parsnip cassoulet

This warming slow-cook winter dish is perfect for casual get-togethers. If friends are late, just turn the oven down to 150C/130C fan/gas 2 and leave for up to 1 hour.

TAKES 2 HOURS • SERVES 6

2 tbsp olive oil
2 large onions, chopped
500g/1lb 2oz pumpkin, seeded, peeled and diced
500g/1lb 2oz parsnips, diced
3 garlic cloves, crushed
2 × 425g cans mixed beans, drained
780g can chopped tomatoes
225ml/8fl oz red wine
300ml/½ pint vegetable stock
2 large fresh thyme sprigs
1 tbsp sugar
85g/3oz fresh breadcrumbs
25g/1oz Parmesan, grated
garlic bread and stir-fried cabbage, to serve

1 Heat oven to 180C/160C fan/gas 4. Heat the oil in a large pan or wok, add the onions, then fry for 5 minutes until golden. Add the pumpkin, parsnips and garlic, and cook for a further 3 minutes. Stir in the beans, tomatoes, wine, stock, thyme, sugar and plenty of seasoning. Bring to the boil, then transfer to a large casserole dish, pressing the beans and vegetables beneath the liquid.

2 Sprinkle the top with the breadcrumbs and grated cheese. Cover, then cook for 40 minutes. Uncover, stir well and cook for a further 40 minutes. Serve with garlic bread and stir-fried cabbage.

PER SERVING 368 kcals, protein 16g, carbs 53g, fat 9g, sat fat 2g, fibre 14g, sugar 3g, salt 2.16g

Veggie lasagne

This light lasagne, packed with vegetables, is topped with a quick crème-fraîche sauce. It includes two of your 5-a-day.

TAKES 1¼ HOURS • SERVES 4

2 tbsp oil
1 onion, sliced
1 garlic clove, sliced
1 aubergine, cut into chunks
1 red pepper, seeded and sliced
8 plum tomatoes, halved
350ml/12fl oz passata
200g/8oz ready-cooked lasagne sheets
6 tbsp half-fat crème fraîche
2 tbsp grated Parmesan

1 Heat oven to 190C/170C fan/gas 5. Toss the oil and vegetables together, and roast in a large shallow roasting tin for 35 minutes until lightly charred.

2 Spoon a layer of roasted veg over the bottom of a medium-sized baking dish. Pour over some passata and cover with a layer of lasagne sheets. Repeat the layers to use up all the roasted veg and passata, finishing with a layer of lasagne. Use a spoon to dollop over the crème fraîche, then sprinkle with the Parmesan.

3 Return to the oven for 25 minutes, until the lasagne is heated through and the top is golden and bubbling.

PER SERVING 279 kcals, protein 9g, carbs 35g, fat 13g, sat fat 4g, fibre 6g, sugar 15g, salt 0.63g

Chickpea & roasted veg stew

This stew tastes even better if it is made a few hours or even a day in advance. Any leftovers can be reheated or frozen.

TAKES 1 HOUR 10 MINUTES
- **SERVES 6**

350g/12oz new potatoes, halved
1 fennel bulb, trimmed and cut into chunks
1 medium carrot, cut into chunks
1 red or yellow pepper, seeded and cut into chunks
1 large red onion, cut into chunks
4 tbsp rapeseed or extra virgin olive oil
1 tsp cumin seeds
1 tsp fennel seeds
1 tsp coriander seeds, crushed
3 garlic cloves, chopped
400g can chopped tomatoes
400g can chickpeas, drained and rinsed
250ml/9fl oz red wine
zest and juice 1 orange
1 cinnamon stick
8 prunes, halved
couscous and toasted flaked almonds, to garnish

1 Heat oven to 220C/200C fan/gas 7. Place the potatoes, fennel, carrot, pepper and onion in a roasting tin with 3 tablespoons of the oil, the cumin, fennel and coriander seeds, and some salt and black pepper. Use your hands to coat everything, then roast for 30 minutes, stirring once, until golden tinged and the potatoes are cooked through.

2 Meanwhile, heat a large pan over a medium heat and add the remaining oil. Fry the garlic until fragrant, then add the tomatoes, chickpeas, wine, orange zest and juice, cinnamon stick and prunes. Bring to the boil and simmer while the vegetables roast. Add the roasted vegetables to the pan and stir. Return to a simmer and cook for 15–20 minutes. Serve over warm couscous scattered with toasted flaked almonds.

PER SERVING 241 kcals, protein 7g, carbs 32g, fat 9g, sat fat 1g, fibre 5g, sugar 15g, salt 0.36g

Onion, walnut & mushroom tarte Tatin

This makes a substantial main course that's full of flavour and can be prepared up to the baking stage a day in advance. Serve with a green salad.

TAKES 1 HOUR 10 MINUTES
- **SERVES 4**

4 onions
3 tbsp olive oil
200g/8oz chestnut mushrooms, halved if large
2 tsp light muscovado sugar
50g/2oz walnut pieces
100g/4oz blue cheese
250g/9oz puff pastry, defrosted if frozen

1 Heat oven to 200C/180C fan/gas 6. Peel the onions and cut each into six wedges through the root. Heat the oil in a large pan, add the onions, then gently fry for 20 minutes until softened and lightly coloured.

2 Add the mushrooms, sugar and some salt and black pepper and give it a good stir. Gently cook, stirring now and then for a further 5 minutes. Stir in the walnuts. Line the base of a 20–23cm sandwich cake tin (not loose-bottomed) with baking parchment. Spoon over the onion mixture and press it down lightly. Crumble over the cheese.

3 Roll out the pastry on a lightly floured work surface and trim it to a round about 5cm larger than the tin. Lay the pastry over the filling and tuck in the ends. Bake for 35–40 minutes until the pastry is crisp and golden. Cool for 5 minutes in the tin, then turn out on to a flat plate and cut into wedges.

PER SERVING 546 kcals, protein 13g, carbs 30g, fat 43g, sat fat 16g, fibre 3g, sugar 9g, salt 1.43g

Golden veggie shepherd's pie

Make this pie then freeze half for another day for up to 2 months. Defrost thoroughly before cooking.

TAKES 2¼ HOURS • SERVES 10

FOR THE LENTIL SAUCE

50g/2oz butter
2 onions, chopped
4 carrots, diced
1 celery head, chopped
4 garlic cloves, finely chopped
200g pack chestnut mushrooms, sliced
2 bay leaves
1 tbsp dried thyme
500g pack dried green lentils
100ml/3½fl oz red wine
1.7 litres/3 pints vegetable stock
3 tbsp tomato purée

FOR THE TOPPING

2kg/4lb 8oz floury potatoes, such as
    King Edward
85g/3oz butter
100ml/3½fl oz milk
50g/2oz Cheddar, grated

1 To make the sauce, heat the butter in a pan, then gently fry the onions, carrots, celery and garlic for 15 minutes until soft and golden. Turn up the heat, add the mushrooms, then cook for 4 minutes more. Stir in the herbs, then add the lentils. Pour over the wine and stock and simmer for 40–50 minutes until the lentils are very soft. Season to taste, take off the heat and stir in the tomato purée.

2 While the lentils are cooking, boil the potatoes for about 15 minutes until tender. Drain well, mash with the butter and milk, then season.

3 Divide the lentil mixture between two dishes and top with mash. Scatter over the cheese and freeze or, if eating that day, heat oven to 190C/170C fan/gas 5, then bake for 30 minutes until the topping is golden.

PER SERVING 449 kcals, protein 19g, carbs 68g, fat 13g, sat fat 7g, fibre 10g, sugar 9g, salt 0.59g

Baked ricotta-stuffed tandoori potatoes

To make garlic or ginger pastes, whizz garlic or ginger in a food processor with a little water. Fresh pastes will keep in an airtight container in the fridge for a week.

TAKES ABOUT 1¼ HOURS

● **SERVES 6**

6 medium potatoes
salad of tomato, onion and coriander leaves, to serve

FOR THE TANDOORI PASTE

150g/5½oz Greek yogurt
1½ tsp each ground garam masala and cumin powder
1½ tsp each garlic and ginger paste
½ tsp ground turmeric
½ tsp red chilli powder
2 tsp lemon juice
1 tbsp vegetable oil

FOR THE FILLING

4 tsp lemon juice (or to taste)
200g/8oz ricotta
3 spring onions, finely sliced
2 green chillies, finely chopped
small bunch of fresh coriander, finely chopped
1½ tsp ground cumin
1¼ tsp freshly ground black pepper
handful of cashew nuts, chopped
4 tsp vegetable oil

1 Heat oven to 190C/170C fan/gas 5. Slice the rounded ends off the potatoes, then use an apple peeler and small knife to hollow them out, leaving a 1–2cm edge all the way around.

2 Mix together the ingredients for the paste and also for the filling in separate bowls, seasoning both mixtures.

3 Fill the potatoes with the ricotta mixture, then coat them in the paste. Sit the potatoes in an ovenproof dish, spoon any remaining paste on top, then cook for 50 minutes–1 hour until the potato is soft when pierced with the tip of a knife. Serve thickly sliced with a salad of tomato, onion and coriander leaves.

PER SERVING 278 kcals, protein 10g, carbs 31g, fat 14g, sat fat 5g, fibre 2g, sugar 3g, salt 1.27g

Squash with rice, sage & goat's cheese

This delicious risotto-like filling combination is slow roasted in the squash to make a wonderful supper dish.

TAKES 1½ HOURS • SERVES 4

2 large butternut squash
2 tbsp olive oil
1 onion, finely chopped
2 garlic cloves, crushed
100g/4oz basmati rice
600ml/1 pint vegetable stock
25g/1oz sundried tomatoes in oil, drained and chopped
100g/4oz firm goat's cheese, roughly chopped
handful of fresh sage leaves, chopped

1 Heat oven to 190C/170C fan/gas 5. Cut the squash in half lengthways, then scoop out the seeds. Brush the insides with a little oil and put in a roasting tin filled to 1cm with water. Roast for around 20–30 minutes until almost tender when tested with a sharp knife. Scoop out some of the flesh and roughly chop.

2 Meanwhile, heat the remaining oil in a pan and cook the onion and garlic for 5 minutes until the onion is tender. Stir in the rice and fry for 1 minute. Add the stock and cook for a further 10–12 minutes until the rice is tender and liquid has all been absorbed. Stir in the chopped squash, tomatoes, goat's cheese, half the sage leaves and a little seasoning.

3 Stuff the squash with filling, top with the remaining sage and cover with foil. Return to the oven and cook for a further 15 minutes until the cheese is melted. Stand for 5 minutes before serving.

PER SERVING 318 kcals, protein 8g, carbs 36g, fat 17g, sat fat 5g, fibre 3g, sugar none, salt 0.84g

Red onion marmalade

This preserve is ideal served with cheese as part of a ploughman's lunch.
Slow cooking is the secret of really soft and sticky onions, so don't rush this part.

TAKES 2–2¼ HOURS, PLUS COOLING
● **MAKES ABOUT 2 LITRES/3½ PINTS**

140g/5oz butter
4 tbsp olive oil
2kg/4lb 8oz red onions, halved and
    thinly sliced
4 garlic cloves, thinly sliced
140g/5oz golden caster sugar
1 tbsp fresh thyme leaves
pinch of chilli flakes (optional)
75cl bottle red wine
350ml/12fl oz sherry vinegar or red
    wine vinegar
200ml/7fl oz port

1 Melt the butter and oil in a large, heavy-based pan over a high heat. Tip in the onions and garlic and give them a good stir so they are glossed with butter. Sprinkle over the sugar, thyme, chilli flakes, if using, and some salt and black pepper. Give everything another really good stir and reduce the heat slightly. Cook uncovered for 40–50 minutes, stirring occasionally. The onions are ready when all their juices have evaporated – they should be soft, sticky and smell of caramelising sugar.

2 Pour in the wine, vinegar and port, and simmer everything, still uncovered, over a high heat for 25–30 minutes, stirring every so often until the onions are a deep mahogany colour and the liquid has reduced by about two-thirds. Leave the onions to cool, then scoop into sterilised jars (see page 144) and seal. Keeps in the fridge for up to 3 months.

PER ROUNDED TBSP 40 kcals, protein 1g, carbs 4g, fat 2g, sat fat 1g, fibre 1g, sugar 4g, salt 0.03g

Fruity chutney

This chutney is as simple as tipping everything into a large pan, letting it all simmer and thicken, then pouring into jars. Its punchy flavours bring out the best in cheese.

TAKES 2 HOURS 10 MINUTES • MAKES ABOUT 2 LITRES/3½ PINTS

900g/2lb plums
2 Bramley apples (about 550g/1lb 4oz)
450g/1lb pears
1 large mango
900g/2lb light muscovado sugar
500ml bottle cider vinegar
2 medium onions, chopped (not red)
85g/3oz chopped stem ginger from a
   jar, drained
3 garlic cloves, finely chopped
1 tbsp mustard seeds
1 rounded tsp ground coriander
1 tsp crushed dried chillies
1 tsp salt
1 cinnamon stick

1 Halve, stone and chop the plums; core, peel and chop the apples and pears; peel, stone and chop the mango. Put all the fruit in a large pan.

2 Stir the sugar, vinegar, onions, ginger, garlic, mustard seeds, coriander, chillies and salt into the pan, then drop the cinnamon stick on top. Heat slowly for about 20 minutes, giving an occasional stir, until the sugar has dissolved. Now leave the chutney to simmer, without a lid, stirring occasionally until reduced and thickened, but still with a nice balance of syrupy juice. This will take about 1½ hours. (Don't cook it until all the liquid has gone, as it will thicken once it cools.) Discard the cinnamon stick.

3 Using a heatproof jug, pour the chutney into sterilised jars (see page 144) while still hot. It will keep for about a year in a cool, dry place.

PER ROUNDED TBSP 57 kcals, protein 1g, carbs 15g, fat 1g, sat fat none, fibre 1g, sugar 12g, salt 0.08g

Pear & dried apricot chutney

This is great for using up a glut of garden fruit. A jar of homemade chutney makes a lovely present for a friend.

TAKES 2 HOURS • MAKES ABOUT 850ML/1½ PINTS

425g/15oz ripe tomatoes, peeled, seeded and chopped

425g/15oz caster sugar

140g/5oz cooking apples, peeled, cored and chopped

140g/5oz onion, finely chopped

140g/5oz dried apricots, chopped

3 tbsp chopped ginger

2 tsp salt

450ml/16fl oz white wine vinegar

1.25kg/2lb 12oz pears, peeled, cored and cut into bite-sized pieces

1 Combine all the ingredients, except the pears, in a large, heavy-bottomed pan, and bring to the boil. Simmer, uncovered, over a very low heat, stirring occasionally with a wooden spoon.

2 Continue to cook for about 1 hour, giving it a stir every 10 minutes until the mixture is syrupy. Add the chopped pears and cook for another 30 minutes, stirring occasionally. Leave until the mixture has cooled completely.

3 Heat oven to 120C/100C fan/gas ½. Wash some jam jars in hot soapy water, rinse well and put on their sides in the oven for 15 minutes. When the jars have cooled, spoon in the chutney and store in a cool, dry place for up to 6 months. It will keep in the fridge for 1 month once opened.

PER ROUNDED TBSP 78 kcals, protein 1g, carbs 20g, fat 1g, sat fat none, fibre 1g, sugar 13g, salt 0.31g

Roast rib of beef with claret & anchovy gravy

For the best flavour, ask your butcher for a well-hung piece of beef (2–3 weeks is optimum). Serve with broccoli or spinach and roast potatoes.

TAKES 2¾–3¼ HOURS • SERVES 8

4-bone rib of beef (about 4.25kg/8–10lb)
1 heaped tbsp plain flour
700ml/1¼ pints hot beef stock
150ml/¼ pint claret
5–6 anchovy fillets in oil, drained and finely snipped
2 heaped tsp Dijon mustard

1 Remove the beef from the fridge at least half an hour before cooking. Calculate the roasting time (17 minutes per 450g/1lb plus 15 minutes for medium–rare meat). Heat oven to 230C/210C fan/gas 8. Season the beef, put in a roasting tin without adding extra fat and roast for 15 minutes.

2 Reduce the oven temperature to 160C/140C fan/gas 3 and roast for the remainder of the calculated time.

3 Transfer the meat to a carving board, cover loosely with foil and set aside to rest for 15 minutes.

4 Pour out all but 2 tablespoons of the fat from the roasting tin. Put the tin on the hob over a medium heat and stir in the flour. Gradually stir in the hot stock, whisking all the time. Whisk in the claret, anchovies and mustard until smooth, then season to taste. Serve alongside the beef.

PER SERVING 914 kcals, protein 88g, carbs 3g, fat 61g, sat fat 27g, fibre 1g, sugar 1g, salt 1.01g

Braised lamb à la grecque

Stuffing is a lovely way to add an intriguing taste to braised meat. The salty feta and the fruity figs combine to make a perfect marriage of flavours with lamb.

TAKES 3 HOURS • SERVES 6–8

8 ready-to-eat dried figs, chopped
200g/8oz feta, chopped
2 garlic cloves, finely chopped
4 tbsp chopped fresh coriander
2 tbsp chopped fresh mint
2kg/4lb 8oz leg of lamb, boned and butterflied (ask the butcher to do this for you)
12 bay leaves
2 tbsp olive oil
4 red onions, thinly sliced
100ml/3½fl oz balsamic vinegar
300ml/½ pint red wine
2 tbsp clear honey

1 Heat oven to 190C/170C fan/gas 5. Mix together the figs, feta, garlic and herbs, and season well. Open out the lamb and scatter over the fig mixture. Fold the lamb back over the stuffing and tie at intervals with string. Slip the bay leaves on top under the string, then season the lamb.

2 Heat the oil in a large flameproof casserole and brown the lamb on all sides. Remove. Add the onions to the dish, and cook for 10–15 minutes, stirring. Add the vinegar, wine and honey, and bubble rapidly for 5 minutes, then put the lamb on top. Cover with a tight-fitting lid and cook for 1½ hours, basting twice with the juices.

3 Remove the lid and cook for around 30 minutes until well browned. Transfer the lamb to a plate, cover with foil, then set aside to rest. If the gravy is a bit thin, bring to the boil and boil hard for 2–3 minutes to reduce and thicken.

PER SERVING (6) 822 kcals, protein 70g, carbs 21g, fat 48g, sat fat 23g, fibre 2g, sugar 5g, salt 1.78g

Duck casserole with herbed new potatoes

Redcurrant jelly and mint give a superb flavour to this non-fatty casserole. Slow cooking means the duck literally falls off the bone when you cut into it.

TAKES 2 HOURS ● SERVES 4

4 duck legs (about 300g/10oz each)
2 tbsp seasoned plain flour
1 tbsp olive oil
1 large onion, thinly sliced
2 garlic cloves, finely chopped
1 tbsp finely chopped fresh rosemary
300ml/½ pint white wine
300ml/½ pint hot chicken stock
500g/1lb 2oz baby new potatoes,
    halved if large
200g/8oz frozen peas
2 tbsp redcurrant jelly
4 tbsp chopped mint leaves

1 Heat oven to 180C/160C fan/gas 4. Dust the duck legs with the seasoned flour. Heat the oil in a wide, shallow casserole dish or large roasting tin, then fry the duck legs until well browned all over. Transfer to a plate. Add the onion, garlic and rosemary to the pan, and cook for about 5 minutes, stirring frequently, until browned. Drain off any excess fat.

2 Return the duck legs to the casserole or tin, then pour in the wine and bubble rapidly for 5 minutes. Add the stock and new potatoes, and cover tightly. Cook in the oven for 1½ hours.

3 Transfer the dish to the hob. Add the peas and redcurrant jelly, and cook for 5 minutes, stirring occasionally, until the jelly has melted. Season with salt and black pepper to taste and stir in the chopped mint.

PER SERVING 494 kcals, protein 38g, carbs 45g, fat 14g, sat fat 3g, fibre 5g, sugar none, salt 0.99g

Chinese tangerine beef casserole

Tangerine peel is a classic Chinese flavouring for braises and other slow-cooked dishes, and it is particularly good with beef.

TAKES 3 HOURS ● SERVES 6

4 tangerines or satsumas
1 tbsp vegetable oil
1kg/2lb 4oz piece topside beef
1 tsp sugar
300ml/ ½ pint beef stock
100ml/3½fl oz soy sauce
100ml/3½fl oz sherry
1 tbsp grated ginger
1 medium onion, sliced
2 star anise
1 tsp Chinese five spice powder
85g/3oz chestnut mushrooms, sliced
85g/3oz shiitake mushrooms, sliced
2 tsp cornflour
egg noodles, to serve
bunch of spring onions, finely
   shredded, to garnish

1 Heat oven to 140C/120C fan/gas 1. Pare the tangerines or satsumas in strips, removing any pith. Put the peel on a baking sheet and bake for 30–45 minutes until crisp and dry but not coloured. Chop and set aside.

2 Increase oven to 160C/140C fan/gas 3. Heat the oil in a flameproof casserole then fry the beef on all sides to seal. Add the sugar, stock, soy sauce, sherry, ginger, onion, star anise, five spice and tangerine peel. Cover tightly and cook for 1¾ hours.

3 Add all the mushrooms and cook for a further 15 minutes. Transfer the beef to a plate to rest.

4 Meanwhile, mix the cornflour with a little water and stir into the casserole. Bring the casserole to the boil on the hob, stirring, then simmer until thickened. Slice the beef and serve with the sauce on a bed of noodles garnished with a few spring onions.

PER SERVING 783 kcals, protein 48g, carbs 77g, fat 32g, sat fat 10g, fibre 1g, sugar 1g, salt 3.91g

Chilli roast pork belly

Belly pork is so full of flavour on its own, but when it gets smothered in this delicious sauce it makes an irresistible dinner-party dish.

TAKES 3½ HOURS • SERVES 6

1.5kg/3lb 5oz piece rolled pork belly
2 tbsp olive oil
3 red chillies, seeded and finely
   chopped
2 garlic cloves, crushed
1 tsp smoked paprika
350ml/12fl oz chicken stock
400g/14oz passata
50ml/2fl oz cider vinegar
85g/3oz light brown soft sugar

1 Heat oven to 180C/160C fan/gas 4. Season the pork well. Heat the oil in a large, deep casserole and brown the pork well on all sides for about 10 minutes. Lift out on to a plate and pour off all but 1 tablespoon of the fat.

2 Return the dish to the heat and fry the chilli and garlic for a few minutes until softened. Stir in the paprika for another minute, then pour in the stock, passata, vinegar and all but 2 tablespoons of the sugar.

3 Rub the remaining sugar over the pork then lower it into the sauce. Cover the pan and roast the pork for 2½–3 hours until it feels tender when pierced with a skewer and the sauce is reduced and sticky.

4 Lift out the pork and let it rest for 10 minutes. Spoon off any excess oil from the casserole and keep the rest of the sauce warm. Serve the pork in thick slices with a little sauce spooned over.

PER SERVING 635 kcals, protein 46g, carbs 20g, fat 42g, sat fat 15g, fibre 1g, sugar 17g, salt 0.84g

Seven-hour lamb

More than 7 hours in the oven, but only a few minutes' work for the cook. This leave-to-cook recipe produces truly melt-in-the-mouth meat.

TAKES 7¾ HOURS • SERVES 6

1 large leg of lamb (about 3kg/6lb 8oz)
drizzle of olive oil (optional)
4 onions, sliced
8 garlic cloves, peeled, but left whole
4 carrots, leave whole if small or
    quarter lengthways
300ml/½ pint white wine
300ml/½ pint stock (use what you
    have)
2 tbsp Armagnac or Madeira (optional)

1 Heat oven to 120C/100C fan/gas ½. Put your largest casserole dish on the hob and brown the seasoned lamb on all sides – do this very thoroughly until it is a good dark brown. If the lamb sticks, add a drizzle of oil. Pour away any fat.

2 Add the vegetables, wine and stock. Season and bring to the boil, then cover and bake for 7 hours, turning twice.

3 There is no need to rest the meat when cooked in this way. Transfer the meat and vegetables to a serving dish, strain the sauce into a jug and blot away any fat with kitchen paper. Pour the sauce into a pan then boil hard to reduce by a quarter – by which time it will be rich and flavoursome. Adjust the seasoning (adding the Armagnac or Madeira, if you wish), and serve alongside the lamb.

PER SERVING 743 kcals, protein 73g, carbs 14g, fat 41g, sat fat 20g, fibre 3g, sugar none, salt 1g

Succulent braised venison

Long, slow cooking tenderises tougher cuts of venison, and vegetables add an earthy sweetness. Don't be tempted to use a lean cut as this will overcook and become dry.

TAKES 2 HOURS • SERVES 8

2 carrots, roughly chopped
140g/5oz turnips or swede, roughly chopped
2 onions, roughly chopped
3 celery sticks, roughly chopped
olive oil and butter, for frying
1 garlic clove, crushed
1kg/2lb 4oz boned leg or shoulder of venison, cut into large chunks (or buy ready-cubed venison for stewing)
5 tbsp seasoned plain flour
2 tbsp redcurrant jelly
450ml/16fl oz dry red wine (Rioja is good)
450ml/16fl oz beef stock
2 fresh thyme sprigs
1 bay leaf

1 Heat oven to 180C/160C fan/gas 4. Fry the vegetables in a little oil and butter in a heavy-based casserole for 4–5 minutes until golden. Tip in the garlic and fry for a further minute, then set aside.
2 Put the venison into a plastic bag with seasoned flour and shake to coat. Add a little more oil and butter to the pan then fry the venison over a high heat, stirring, until well browned – cook it in batches if necessary. Set aside with the vegetables.
3 Add the redcurrant jelly and wine to the pan, and bring to the boil, scraping up all the bits that have stuck to the bottom. Pour in the stock, then add the thyme, bay leaf, meat and vegetables. Season and bring to the boil. Cover and transfer to the oven for about 1½ hours or until tender. Remove from the oven and check the seasoning.

PER SERVING 277 kcals, protein 30g, carbs 18g, fat 10g, sat fat 2g, fibre 2g, sugar 2g, salt 0.7g

Spicy beef with pumpkin & corn

This casserole is mildly spiced, but for those who like extra heat, put the bottle of Tabasco on the table, so that they can pep up their own serving.

TAKES ABOUT 2¾ HOURS • SERVES 6

1.3kg/3lb braising beef
1 tbsp seasoned plain flour
2 tbsp olive oil
2 onions, sliced
2 garlic cloves, chopped
850ml/1½ pints beef or vegetable stock
2 tbsp tomato purée
1 tbsp paprika
2 tsp dried oregano
900g/2lb pumpkin
3 corn on the cob
1 tsp Tabasco, plus extra to taste
chopped fresh parsley, to garnish

1 Cut the beef into 4cm chunks and toss in the seasoned flour. Heat the oil in a large pan with a tightly fitting lid. Add the beef, in batches if necessary, and fry on all sides until browned. Add the onions and garlic, and stir well. Cook for about 5 minutes.

2 Stir in the stock, tomato purée, paprika and oregano. Bring to the boil, then cover tightly and simmer for 1½ hours.

3 Meanwhile, peel and seed the pumpkin. Cut into 4cm chunks, add to the casserole and return to the boil. Cook for a further 30 minutes. Cut the corn across into 4cm slices and add to the casserole along with the Tabasco. Cook for a further 10–15 minutes, then taste and adjust the seasoning and sprinkle with parsley.

PER SERVING 433 kcals, protein 52g, carbs 18g, fat 18g, sat fat 6g, fibre 3g, sugar none, salt 1.16g

Braised lamb shanks

Slow-cooked, meaty dishes like this are always a hit with guests. The shanks can be braised up to 2 days ahead, then reheated in the sauce.

TAKES 2 HOURS 40 MINUTES

● **SERVES 8**

2 tbsp olive oil
8 lamb shanks
1 onion, roughly chopped
2 carrots, roughly chopped
few fresh rosemary sprigs
3 fresh bay leaves
4 garlic cloves, left whole
2 tbsp plain flour
1 tbsp tomato purée
350ml/12fl oz white wine
500ml/18fl oz lamb or chicken stock

1 Heat oven to 200C/180C fan/gas 6. Pour the oil in a casserole dish or roasting tin large enough to fit all the shanks. Put the dish or tin on the hob and spend a good 10 minutes browning the lamb all over. Remove the lamb, then add the onion and carrots, and cook for 10 minutes until starting to brown.

2 Stir in the herbs and garlic, and cook for a few minutes more. Stir in the flour and tomato purée, season well, return the lamb to the dish, then pour over the wine and stock. Bring to a simmer, cover tightly with a lid or foil and cook in the oven for 1½–2 hours until the lamb is tender.

3 Remove the lamb from the sauce and set aside. Put the dish back on the hob and let the sauce bubble down for about 15 minutes until rich and glossy, then pass the sauce through a sieve. To serve, reheat the lamb in the sauce, adding a splash of water if it is too thick.

PER SERVING 295 kcals, protein 25g, carbs 5g, fat 18g, sat fat 8g, fibre none, sugar 2g, salt 0.41g

Oven-poached salmon with pepper & basil sauce

Buy the fish according to the length of your roasting tin, removing the head and most of the tail to fit it in.

TAKES 1½ HOURS ● SERVES 6

1 whole salmon(about 1.5–2kg/3lb 5oz–4lb 8oz), gutted

FOR THE COURT BOUILLON

250ml/9fl oz dry white wine

3 tbsp white wine vinegar

1 small lemon, sliced

1 medium onion, sliced

1 carrot, chopped

2 bay leaves

2 sprigs each fresh tarragon and thyme

½ tsp whole black peppercorns

FOR THE SAUCE

2 roasted red peppers from a jar, finely chopped

1 shallot, finely chopped

5 tbsp olive oil

6 basil sprigs, stems chopped, leaves left whole

1 tbsp balsamic or sherry vinegar

100ml/3½fl oz dry white wine

1 Heat oven to 160C/140C fan/gas 3. Put the court bouillon ingredients in a pan with 1.5 litres/2¾ pints water. Bring to the boil and simmer for 20 minutes.

2 Strain the liquor over the fish in the roasting tin, cover tightly with foil and cook in the oven (30 minutes per kg/ 13 minutes per lb).

3 Sauté the peppers and shallot in the oil for 5 minutes. Add the chopped basil stems, vinegar, wine and seasoning. Simmer for another 10 minutes. Tear most of the basil leaves into pieces and scatter over the sauce.

4 Remove the fish from the oven and uncover it, leaving it in the liquor for 15 minutes. Carefully lift the fish on to a board, peel off the skin and scrape away the brown flesh as neatly as possible.

5 Slide the fish on to a platter, then spoon some sauce on top, sprinkle with the remaining basil leaves and serve with the rest of the sauce in a bowl.

PER SERVING 439 kcals, protein 32g, carbs 3g, fat 29g, sat fat 5g, fibre 1g, sugar none, salt 0.57g

Slow-roasted pork with fennel

Here's a scrummy new way to cook pork. Serve simply with a winter green salad and braised cannellini beans.

TAKES 2½ HOURS, PLUS MARINATING
- **SERVES 8**

2kg/4lb 8oz rolled boned pork shoulder joint
3 garlic cloves, finely chopped
1 tbsp fennel seeds, crushed
1 tbsp black peppercorns, crushed
1 tbsp chopped fresh rosemary leaves
2 bay leaves, finely chopped
300ml/½ pint dry white wine

1 Cut the string from the joint and unroll it. Flatten out as much as possible, cutting through any thick pieces if necessary to give you an even thickness of meat. Mix together the garlic, fennel, peppercorns, rosemary, bay leaves and 1 teaspoon salt. Sprinkle evenly over all sides of the pork and massage it in. Put on a platter, cover loosely with foil and chill for at least 4 hours or up to 24 hours.

2 Re-roll the joint and tie at intervals along its length with string. Bring to room temperature an hour before roasting.

3 Heat oven to 180C/160C fan/gas 4. Roast the pork in a roasting tin for 2 hours, basting occasionally and adding the wine after 1 hour. When cooked, remove from the oven, transfer to a serving platter and pour over the pan juices. Cover tightly with foil and leave to rest for 15 minutes before serving.

PER SERVING 436 kcals, protein 44g, carbs 3g, fat 26g, sat fat 10g, fibre none, sugar 2g, salt 0.94g

Roast duck legs with red wine sauce

Long, slow roasting is the perfect way to cook duck legs, as the flesh falls off the bones and the fat is released into the gravy to add body and flavour.

TAKES 1 HOUR 20 MINUTES
- **SERVES 4**

4 duck legs
bunch of fresh rosemary sprigs
4 fat garlic cloves
½ tsp five spice powder
½ × 75cl bottle red wine
2 tbsp redcurrant jelly

1 Heat oven to 190C/170C fan/gas 5. Put the duck legs in one layer in a roasting tin on a bed of rosemary sprigs and garlic cloves. Sprinkle with salt and the five spice powder. Roast for 1 hour.

2 About 10 minutes before the end of the cooking time, bring the wine and jelly to a gentle simmer in a pan, stirring to dissolve the jelly, then continue to simmer for 5 minutes.

3 Remove the duck from the oven and spoon off almost all the fat, then pour the wine mixture around it and return it to the oven for 10–15 minutes to finish cooking and to reduce the sauce.

PER SERVING 473 kcals, protein 48g, carbs 7g, fat 20g, sat fat 6g, fibre 1g, sugar 3g, salt 0.51g

Chicken & olive casserole

Full of Mediterranean flavours, this is perfect for outdoor summer dinner parties. You can make this a day ahead, but don't add the olives, mozzarella or basil until the day.

TAKES 2 HOURS ● SERVES 6

1 tbsp olive oil

6 skinless boneless chicken breasts, each cut into 3–4 pieces

3 red peppers, seeded and cut into chunks

2 onions, chopped

8 rashers smoked back bacon, cut into strips

2 garlic cloves, finely chopped

3 tbsp chopped oregano

690g jar passata

50g/2oz pitted black olives

2 × 150g mozzarella balls, cubed

basil leaves, shredded, to garnish

buttered noodles, to serve

1 Heat oven to 180C/160C fan/gas 4. Heat the oil in a flameproof casserole. Add the chicken and peppers, and brown all over, then remove. Add the onions and bacon, and cook for 10 minutes, adding the garlic and oregano for the last minute.

2 Return the chicken and peppers to the pan with the passata. Cover and cook in the oven for 1 hour. Add the olives, then cook for 30 minutes more until the chicken is cooked through and really tender. Remove from the oven and stir in the mozzarella. Season to taste. Sprinkle over the basil and serve with a helping of buttered noodles.

PER SERVING 600 kcals, protein 48g, carbs 16g, fat 39g, sat fat 15g, fibre 3g, sugar 4g, salt 3.4g

Pot-roasted brisket with pancetta & red wine

The long cooking gives this dish a really good, deep flavour and beautifully textured, melt-in-the-mouth beef.

TAKES 3¼ HOURS • SERVES 6-8

1.8kg/4lb boned and rolled brisket of beef

85g/3oz pancetta, chopped

2 garlic cloves, cut into thin slivers

1 tsp chopped fresh thyme, plus a few whole sprigs

3 tbsp olive oil

400g/14oz baby onions or shallots

450g/1lb young carrots

2–3 celery sticks, finely chopped

75cl bottle fruity red wine

2–3 bay leaves

2 tbsp tomato purée

1 tsp light muscovado sugar

1 Wipe the meat dry. Season. Mix together half the pancetta, the garlic, chopped thyme and ½ teaspoon salt. Make deep incisions in the beef and push in the mixture with a spoon handle.

2 Heat oven to 180C/160C fan/gas 4. Heat the oil in a flameproof casserole dish and brown the beef all over. Remove and set aside. Add the onions, brown, then remove. Reduce the heat and cook the remaining pancetta with half of the carrots and the celery for 6 minutes.

3 Return the beef to the pan with the wine, thyme sprigs, bay, purée and sugar. Bring to a simmer, cover and roast in the oven for 1¾ hours, turning once.

4 Remove from the oven and add the onions and remaining carrots, finely chopped. Cover and cook for 50 minutes.

5 Put the vegetables and meat on a serving dish, cover loosely with foil and leave for 10 minutes. Boil the juices in the dish to thicken and season to serve.

PER SERVING 751 kcals, protein 59g, carbs 9g, fat 44g, sat fat 17g, fibre 3g, sugar 1g, salt 0.87g

Easy cassoulet

The traditional cassoulet from southwest France is a long, complicated affair. This rich and tasty version, however, couldn't be simpler!

TAKES 2 HOURS 10 MINUTES

- **SERVES 6**

1 tbsp olive oil

25g/1oz butter

400g pack spicy pork and garlic
    sausages, cut into 4cm/1½in pieces
    (we used Toulouse sausages)

700g/1lb 9oz boneless shoulder of
    pork, trimmed and cut into 4cm/1½in
    pieces

2 onions, thinly sliced

2 garlic cloves, roughly chopped

1 × 400g can chopped tomatoes, plus
    1 × 230g can

300ml/½ pint red wine

2 tbsp tomato purée

1 bay leaf

1 tbsp fresh thyme leaves or 1½tsp
    dried

2 × 400g cans cannellini beans, drained

FOR THE TOPPING

85g/3oz fresh white breadcrumbs

large handful of chopped fresh parsley

1 tbsp olive oil

1 Heat oven to 180C/160C fan/gas 4. Heat the oil and butter in a large flameproof casserole dish and fry the sausages for 4–5 minutes until browned. Remove from the dish and set aside.

2 Fry the pork in the casserole dish for 8–10 minutes, until browned. Remove and set aside. Tip in the onions and fry for 3–4 minutes, then add the garlic and cook, stirring, for a few minutes more.

3 Return the sausages and pork to the pan, and pour in the tomatoes, wine and purée. Add the bay leaf and thyme, and season to taste. Stir well and bring to a gentle simmer. Cover, transfer to the oven and cook for 1 hour.

4 Remove the casserole from the oven and stir in the beans. Return to the oven, uncovered, for 30 minutes.

5 Preheat the grill to high. Mix together the breadcrumbs and parsley, then sprinkle over the cassoulet. Drizzle over the oil and grill until golden.

PER SERVING 583 kcals, protein 46g, carbs 31g, fat 28g, sat fat 4g, fibre 6g, sugar none, salt 3.39g

Salt-crust sirloin with roasted beetroot

The flavour of the beef is crucial to the success of this dish, so do order good-quality meat from a reliable butcher or meat counter.

TAKES 3½ HOURS • SERVES 6

12 small young beetroot
2 tbsp olive oil
1.5kg/3lb 5oz piece boneless sirloin
1 tbsp Maldon sea salt
3 tbsp horseradish sauce
200ml pot crème fraîche
2 tbsp chopped fresh parsley and
  2 tbsp snipped fresh chives, to
  garnish

1 Heat oven to 180C/160C fan/gas 4. Trim the beetroot, scrub well and pat dry with kitchen paper. Tip them into a roasting tin and toss in half the oil. Bake for 2 hours until tender, then set aside.
2 Sprinkle the meat with the sea salt and some black pepper. Heat the remaining oil until very hot in a large frying pan, then sear meat until evenly browned. Transfer to another roasting tin and roast for 40–50 minutes for medium.
3 Remove from the oven, set on a board, cover with foil and rest for around 10 minutes. Return the beetroot to the oven to reheat for 10 minutes. Mix the horseradish with the crème fraîche and season.
4 To serve, thinly slice the beef and arrange on warmed plates. Cut each beetroot almost in half and set two on each plate beside the beef. Spoon horseradish cream on top and sprinkle with the parsley and chives.

PER SERVING 611 kcals, protein 59g, carbs 8g, fat 38g, sat fat 17g, fibre 2g, sugar 1g, salt 2.29g

Slow-roast Persian lamb with pomegranate salad

The pomegranate salad is also delicious on its own with some crumbled feta.
Pomegranate molasses is available from the special products section in supermarkets.

TAKES 3 HOURS 50 MINUTES

● **SERVES 6**

FOR THE LAMB

4 tbsp pomegranate molasses
1 tsp ground cumin
juice of 1 lemon
1 tbsp olive oil
2 garlic cloves, minced
1 onion, roughly chopped
1 shoulder of lamb (about 1.6kg/3lb
   8oz), lightly scored

FOR THE SALAD

seeds of 2 pomegranates
handful of fresh flat-leaf parsley leaves
100g bag watercress
1 small red onion, finely diced
1 tbsp olive oil
warmed flatbreads, to serve

1 Heat oven to 160C/140C fan/gas 3. In a small bowl, mix the molasses with the cumin, lemon juice, oil and garlic. Scatter the onion over the base of a casserole dish or deep roasting tin. Place the lamb on top of the onions. Pour the molasses glaze over the lamb then rinse out the bowl with about 200ml/7fl oz water and pour it around – not over – the lamb.

2 Cover the dish with a lid or the tin with a large piece of foil. Roast the lamb, undisturbed, for 3 hours, then remove the lid or foil and continue to roast for 30 minutes to give the lamb colour. Pour off the juices, remove as much fat as possible, then pour the juices back over the lamb.

3 Just before serving, gently toss together all the salad ingredients. Serve the lamb with its sauce, the salad and some warmed flatbreads.

PER SERVING 554 kcals, protein 37g, carbs 15g, fat 39g, sat fat 18g, fibre 2g, sugar 13g, salt 0.35g

Sticky date pudding with caramel sauce

A satisfyingly sticky dessert. Use Medjool dates if you can, as they are large, soft and succulently sweet with a delicious fruity flavour.

TAKES 2¼ HOURS ● SERVES 8

175g/6oz dates
100g/4oz softened butter, plus extra for
  greasing
100g/4oz light muscovado sugar
2 eggs, lightly beaten
½ tsp vanilla extract
175g/6oz self-raising flour, plus
  1 rounded tbsp
4 tbsp milk

FOR THE SAUCE

140g/5oz light muscovado sugar
142ml pot double cream
100g/4oz butter
½ tsp vanilla extract

1 Butter a 1.4-litre pudding basin. Halve, stone and chop the dates.

2 In a bowl, beat together the butter and sugar until light and fluffy. Beat in the eggs, a little at a time. Add the vanilla, then fold in the flour and milk to form a soft dropping consistency. Stir in the chopped dates.

3 Spoon the mixture into the pudding basin and smooth the top. Cover with a piece of buttered greaseproof paper, then a piece of foil, making a pleat in the centre of each to allow the pudding to rise. Tie the cover securely with string, then put in a steamer or large pan containing enough gently simmering water to come halfway up the sides of the basin. Steam for 2 hours until risen and firm.

4 Put all the sauce ingredients in a small pan and bring to the boil, stirring. Simmer for 5 minutes until thickened. Serve with the pudding.

PER SERVING 498 kcals, protein 5g, carbs 54g, fat 31g, sat fat 19g, fibre 1g, sugar 31g, salt 0.78g

Cranberry pud with white-chocolate sauce

If you can't get hold of ground rice, use self-raising flour instead for this tasty pud.

TAKES ABOUT 2 HOURS • SERVES 8

FOR THE TOPPING

140g/5oz fresh or frozen cranberries
200g jar redcurrant jelly
50g/2oz caster sugar

FOR THE SPONGE

175g/6oz self-raising flour
50g/2oz ground rice
1 tsp baking powder
200g/8oz golden caster sugar
4 eggs
seeds from a vanilla pod
200g/8oz butter, plus extra for greasing

FOR THE CUSTARD SAUCE

100g/4oz white chocolate, chopped
500ml pot fresh vanilla custard

1 Put 100g/4oz of the cranberries in a pan with the redcurrant jelly and the sugar, simmer for 5 minutes and cool.

2 Beat together the sponge ingredients then stir in the remaining cranberries. Spoon a third of the cranberry and redcurrant jelly mix into a buttered 1.4-litre pudding basin, then spoon the sponge mix on top.

3 Cover with buttered baking paper and top with foil. Secure it with string, leaving a little room to allow the pudding to rise, then put in a steamer or pan containing enough simmering water to come halfway up the sides of the basin. Cook, covered, for 1½ hours.

4 Put the chocolate into a microwave-proof bowl, add the custard and heat in the microwave according to the packet instructions, stirring occasionally.

5 To serve, reheat the remaining cranberry mix and pour over the turned-out pudding, with the custard alongside.

PER SERVING 650 kcals, protein 9g, carbs 88g, fat 32g, sat fat 19g, fibre 1g, sugar 64g, salt 1g

Squidgy lemon–ginger cake

Store your root ginger in a freezer bag in the freezer and grate it straight from frozen for ease. If well wrapped, the cake keeps for at least a week.

TAKES 2 HOURS • CUTS INTO 12 SLICES

200g/8oz butter, cut in pieces, plus extra for greasing
200g/8oz dates, stoned
300g/10oz dark muscovado sugar
2 eggs
50g/2oz fresh or frozen ginger, grated
grated zest of 1 lemon
200g/8oz self-raising flour
1 Bramley apple (about 250g/9oz), peeled and chopped into pea-sized pieces
50g/2oz white chocolate
1 tbsp chopped candied lemon peel and 1 tbsp sugar 'coffee crystals', to decorate

1 Heat oven to 160C/140C fan/gas 3. Butter and line a 20cm-round cake tin (about 8cm deep) with baking parchment. Put the dates in a bowl and cover with boiling water. Heat the butter in a small pan until melted, then stir in the sugar. Allow to cool slightly. Beat in the eggs, ginger and lemon zest.

2 Drain the dates and chop them finely. Scrape them into the pan too and mix well. Stir in the flour, then the apple. Spoon into the cake tin, put the tin on a baking sheet and bake for about 1¼ hours, until well risen. A skewer inserted into the centre of the cake should come out with a few moist crumbs sticking to it. Leave to cool in the tin.

3 Break the white chocolate into a bowl and melt in the microwave. Trickle the chocolate over the cake, scatter with candied peel and coffee crystals.

PER SLICE 376 kcals, protein 4g, carbs 57g, fat 16g, sat fat 9g, fibre 2g, sugar 30g, salt 0.53g

Bramley & blackberry tray cake

This is like a right-way-up upside-down cake. You don't need special equipment for this, simply use a medium-sized roasting tin – the perfect size is 30 × 20cm.

TAKES 1½ HOURS ● SERVES 8

175g/6oz butter, plus extra for greasing
300g/10oz plain flour, plus extra for
    dusting
4 Bramley apples (about 800g/1lb 12oz)
squeeze of lemon juice
284ml pot whipping cream
200g/8oz golden caster sugar, plus
    1 tbsp for sprinkling
3 eggs
300g/10oz blackberries

1 Heat oven to 200C/180C fan/gas 6. Grease a roasting tin with butter, dust with a little flour, then set aside. Peel, core and slice the apples into rings, then toss them in a little lemon juice to stop them going brown.

2 Tip the cream and butter into a pan, bring to the boil, then set aside. Whisk the sugar with the eggs for about 3 minutes until they thicken and turn pale. Whisk the buttery cream into the eggs, then fold in the flour until the mixture is completely smooth.

3 Pour the batter into the prepared tin and arrange the apple slices over the top. Scatter over the blackberries, then sprinkle with the remaining sugar. Bake for 50 minutes–1 hour until golden and beginning to pull away from the sides of the tin. Leave to cool in the tin and serve cut into squares.

PER SERVING 587 kcals, protein 7g, carbs 64g, fat 35g, sat fat 21g, fibre 3g, sugar 42g, salt 1.01g

Pears roasted in red wine

This is so simple – a lot easier than all the hassle of peeling the pears, then poaching them on the hob. And it's low in fat, too.

TAKES 1 HOUR 20 MINUTES
● SERVES 6

6–8 Comice pears
250ml/9fl oz red wine
50g/2oz cold butter
100g/4oz demerara sugar
2 cinnamon sticks, broken in half
2 star anise
mascarpone, to serve

1 Heat oven to 200C/180C fan/gas 6. Cut a small slice off the bottom of each pear so they sit up. Put the pears into a casserole dish and pour over the wine. Cut the butter into cubes and push a cube on to the top of each pear. Sprinkle over the sugar, scatter in the cinnamon and star anise. Cover with a lid or foil, then bake in the oven for 30 minutes.

2 Remove the pears from the oven, baste them well in their juices, then return to the oven, uncovered and basting occasionally, for 40 minutes until the pears are soft and wrinkled. The pears can be prepared to this point up to 2 days ahead then reheated in a low oven.

3 Serve the pears warm with their juices and a spoonful of mascarpone.

PER SERVING 191 kcals, protein 1g, carbs 30g, fat 7g, sat fat 4g, fibre 3g, sugar 30g, salt 0.16g

Bread pudding

This simple bake is lovely with custard or ice cream for dessert or even with a cup of tea. Perfect for using up any leftover bread.

TAKES 2 HOURS • CUTS INTO 9 SQUARES

500g/1lb 2oz white or wholemeal bread
500g/1lb 2oz dried mixed fruit
85g/3oz mixed peel
1½ tbsp ground mixed spice
600ml/1 pint milk
2 eggs, beaten
140g/5oz light muscovado sugar
zest of 1 lemon (optional)
100g/4oz butter, melted
2 tbsp demerara sugar

1 Tear the bread into a large mixing bowl and add the fruit, peel and mixed spice. Pour in the milk, then stir or scrunch through your fingers to mix everything well and completely break up the bread. Add the eggs, muscovado and lemon zest, if using. Stir well, then set aside for 15 minutes to soak.

2 Heat oven to 180C/160C fan/gas 4. Butter and line the base of a non-stick 20cm-square cake tin (not one with a loose base). Stir the melted butter into the pudding mixture, tip into the tin, then scatter with the demerara. Bake for 1½ hours until firm and golden, covering with foil if it starts to brown too much. Turn out of the tin and strip off the paper. Cut into squares and serve warm.

PER SQUARE 510 kcals, protein 10g, carbs 94g, fat 13g, sat fat 7g, fibre 3g, sugar 67g, salt 1.15g

Heavenly chocolate pudding

Easy to make and a surefire winner – who could resist a steamed chocolate pud topped with a rich chocolate sauce?

TAKES 1½ HOURS • SERVES 6

100g/4oz butter, plus extra for greasing
2 tbsp golden syrup
100g/4oz dark muscovado sugar
150ml/¼ pint milk
1 egg
1 heaped tbsp cocoa powder
200g/8oz self-raising flour
1 tsp ground cinnamon
¼ tsp bicarbonate of soda

FOR THE CHOCOLATE SAUCE

4 tbsp milk
4 tbsp cream
1 tbsp golden syrup
100g/4oz good-quality dark chocolate

1 Butter the inside of a 1.2-litre pudding bowl and line the base with a disc of buttered greaseproof paper.

2 Melt the butter, syrup and sugar in a pan. Remove from the heat and stir in the milk and egg. Add the cocoa to the flour, then tip this mixture into the pan with the cinnamon and bicarbonate of soda.

3 Pour the mixture into the pudding bowl, cover tightly with foil and steam for 1¼ hours. Just before the end, heat the sauce ingredients until melted, stirring all the time.

4 Turn out the pudding (run a knife around the inside of the bowl if necessary) and discard the paper disc. Pour the sauce over the top and serve straight away.

PER SERVING 507 kcals, protein 8g, carbs 65g, fat 26g, sat fat 15g, fibre 2g, sugar 31g, salt 0.9g

Apricot, almond & ricotta cake

This irresistible cake has the lightness of a sponge but the richness of a cheesecake. The cake base can also be used for peaches, nectarines or plums.

TAKES 1 HOUR 50 MINUTES • CUTS INTO 10 SLICES

250g pot ricotta
140g/5oz butter, melted, plus extra for greasing
4 eggs, beaten
200g/8oz golden caster sugar, plus 1 tbsp for the topping
250g/9oz self-raising flour
200g pack ground almonds
4 tbsp apricot jam
5 apricots, stoned and quartered
handful of flaked almonds
icing sugar, to dust

1 Heat oven to 190C/170C fan/gas 5. In a bowl beat the ricotta, butter, eggs and sugar together, then fold in the flour and ground almonds. Spoon half the batter into a greased and lined 22cm-round cake tin. Evenly blob the jam over the middle, then cover this jam with the remaining batter.

2 Arrange the apricot quarters over the top. Scatter over the flaked almonds and remaining caster sugar, then bake for 1½ hours until risen and golden and the apricots have shrivelled and caramelised. Leave the cake to cool slightly, then remove from the tin and leave to cool on a wire rack. Dust with icing sugar and serve cut in slices.

PER SLICE 516 kcals, protein 13g, carbs 53g, fat 30g, sat fat 11g, fibre 3g, sugar 33g, salt 0.61g

Sugar-crusted bara brith

This is the classic Welsh fruity tea bread. Try a slice spread with butter, toasted, or just as it is for a teatime treat.

TAKES 1¼–1½ HOURS, PLUS SOAKING
- **SERVES 12**

400g/14oz luxury dried mixed fruit
75g pack dried cranberries (or extra mixed fruit)
1 mug hot strong black tea
100g/4oz butter, plus extra for greasing
2 heaped tbsp orange marmalade
2 eggs, beaten
450g/1lb self-raising flour (try a mix of wholemeal and white)
175g/6oz light brown soft sugar
1 tsp each ground cinnamon and ground ginger
4 tbsp milk, plus optional extra
50g/2oz crushed sugar cubes or granulated sugar, to decorate

1 Mix together the dried fruit and cranberries in a bowl, then pour over the hot tea. Cover with cling film and leave to soak overnight.

2 Heat oven to 180C/160C fan/gas 4. Butter and line the base of a 900g loaf tin. Melt the butter and marmalade together in a pan, leave to cool for 5 minutes, then beat in the eggs.

3 Strain any excess tea from the fruit. Mix together the flour, sugar and spices, then stir in the fruit, butter mix and milk until evenly combined. The batter should softly drop from the spoon – add more milk if needed.

4 Spoon the mix into the tin and level the top. Sprinkle with the crushed sugar and bake for 1–1¼ hours until dark golden and a skewer inserted in the centre comes out clean. Cover loosely with foil if it starts to over-colour before the middle is cooked. Leave to cool completely in the tin.

PER SERVING 397 kcals, protein 6g, carbs 79g, fat 9g, sat fat 5g, fibre 2g, sugar 50g, salt 0.58g

Caramel-apple loaf cake

This scrummy cake is topped with a sensational toffee sauce and crunchy walnuts. The cake can be frozen without the topping.

TAKES 1 HOUR 50 MINUTES • CUTS INTO 8-10 SLICES

175g/6oz soft butter, plus extra for greasing
175g/6oz golden caster sugar
1 tsp vanilla extract
2 eggs
200g/8oz plain flour
½ tsp ground cinnamon
4 rounded tbsp Greek yogurt
2 eating apples
50g/2oz walnuts, very roughly chopped, plus 1 tbsp extra, chopped
50g/2oz soft toffees
2 tbsp double cream

1 Heat oven to 160C/140C fan/gas 3. Grease a 900g loaf tin and line the base and ends with a long strip of baking paper.

2 Beat together the butter, sugar and vanilla until pale, then beat in the eggs, one by one. Tip in the flour, cinnamon and yogurt. Peel, core and chop the apples into small chunks, then add to the bowl and mix everything together.

3 Scrape into the tin, smooth the top and scatter walnuts down the middle. Bake on a middle shelf for 1 hour 20 minutes–1½ hours until a skewer inserted in the centre comes out clean. Cool in the tin.

4 Gently heat the toffees and cream in a pan and stir until melted into a smooth caramel sauce. Cool for 1 minute while you gently turn out the cake. Slowly drizzle the sauce over the cake. Scatter with extra walnuts. Leave for 10 minutes before serving.

PER SLICE 490 kcals, protein 7g, carbs 53g, fat 29g, sat fat 15g, fibre 2g, sugar 30g, salt 0.64g

Slow-baked clotted cream rice pudding

Homemade rice pudding is great – try this version and fall back in love with one of the best comfort foods there is.

TAKES ABOUT 1½ HOURS • SERVES 4

25g/1oz butter, plus extra for greasing
100g/4oz pudding rice
450ml/16fl oz full-fat milk
284ml pot double cream
227g pot clotted cream
1 split vanilla pod
85g/3oz golden caster sugar
freshly grated nutmeg
raspberry jam, to serve

1 Heat oven to 180C/160C fan/gas 4. Lightly butter a shallow ovenproof dish. Wash the rice well under cold water in a sieve and leave to drain. Bring the milk and creams to the boil in a pan with the vanilla pod, add the rice and sugar, then stir well.

2 Tip the rice into the prepared dish then grate a little nutmeg over the top. Dot with knobs of butter then bake in the oven for 15 minutes. Lower the oven to 160C/140C fan/gas 3, then bake for 1 hour more, by which time the pudding should be golden brown on top and creamy underneath. Serve with large spoonfuls of raspberry jam.

PER SERVING 972 kcals, protein 8g, carbs 49g, fat 84g, sat fat 50g, fibre none, sugar 30g, salt 0.29g

Schooldays treacle sponge

Some dishes come and go, but classic British puds are always popular. Here's a favourite that's even better than you remember.

TAKES 2 HOURS • SERVES 4

175g/6oz unsalted butter, softened, plus extra for greasing
3 tbsp golden syrup, plus optional extra for drizzling
1 tbsp fresh white breadcrumbs
splash of brandy (optional, but delicious)
175g/6oz golden caster sugar
zest of 1 lemon
3 eggs, beaten
175g/6oz self-raising flour
2 tbsp milk
clotted cream, to serve

1 Use a small knob of butter to heavily grease a 1-litre pudding basin. In a small bowl, mix the golden syrup with the breadcrumbs and brandy, if using, then tip into the pudding basin.

2 Beat the butter with the sugar and lemon zest until light and fluffy, then add the eggs gradually. Fold in the flour, then finally add the milk.

3 Spoon the mix into the pudding basin and cover with a double layer of buttered foil and baking paper, making a pleat in the centre to allow the pudding to rise. Tie the cover securely with string, then place in a steamer or large pan containing enough gently simmering water to come halfway up the sides of the basin. Steam for 1½ hours.

4 Turn out the pudding on to a serving dish and serve with lashings of clotted cream and a little extra golden syrup drizzled over, if you wish.

PER SERVING 763 kcals, protein 10g, carbs 90g, fat 43g, sat fat 25g, fibre 1g, sugar 56g, salt 0.71g

Pineapple & stem ginger pudding

This pud's made from storecupboard ingredients. Serve with custard made with coconut milk instead of milk to complement the Caribbean flavours.

TAKES 2 HOURS 20 MINUTES
- **SERVES 8**

15g/½oz butter, softened
432g can pineapple chunks in juice, drained
100g/4oz golden syrup
100g/4oz plain flour
100g/4oz vegetable suet
100g/4oz fresh white breadcrumbs
4 tsp ground ginger
4 tsp ground mixed spice
2 tsp baking powder
2 tsp bicarbonate of soda
275ml/9½fl oz milk, warmed
12 pieces (about 175g/6oz) stem ginger in syrup, drained and roughly chopped
1 medium egg, beaten
coconut custard, to serve (optional)

1 Butter a 1.4-litre pudding basin. Line the base with a disc of greaseproof paper. Put the pineapple in the basin and pour in the golden syrup.

2 In a large bowl, mix together the flour, suet, breadcrumbs, ginger, mixed spice, baking powder and bicarbonate of soda. Stir in the milk, stem ginger and egg, and beat until well combined. Pour over the pineapple. Cover the basin with a double layer of pleated greaseproof paper. Cover with a pleated layer of foil and secure with string.

3 Stand the pudding basin on an upturned saucer in a large pan and pour in enough boiling water to come halfway up the sides of the basin. Bring to the boil, cover, and simmer for 2 hours, adding extra boiling water if necessary. Turn out the pudding onto a serving plate. Serve immediately with coconut custard, if you like.

PER SERVING 357 kcals, protein 6g, carbs 49g, fat 17g, sat fat 8g, fibre 1g, sugar 12g, salt 1.25g

Cherry & almond cake

This cake will keep moist for up to 3 days, wrapped tightly in cling film and overwrapped in foil. Or it can be frozen for 3 months.

TAKES 1½ HOURS ● CUTS INTO 12 SLICES

200g/8oz softened butter, plus extra to grease
100g pack blanched almonds, toasted
225g/8½oz golden caster sugar
3 eggs
200g/8oz self-raising flour
250g/9oz glacé cherries, halved
50g/2oz flaked almonds

1 Heat oven to 180C/160C fan/gas 4. Butter the base and sides of a deep 20cm-round cake tin, then line the base with baking paper.

2 Tip the toasted almonds into a food processor and whizz until finely ground. Beat together the butter and sugar in a large bowl with an electric hand whisk until pale and fluffy. Add the eggs one at a time with a little of the flour, beating well between each addition. Carefully fold in the ground toasted almonds and remaining flour.

3 Gently stir in the cherries until they are evenly distributed. Spoon the mixture into the tin and smooth the top. Cover with flaked almonds then bake the cake in the centre of the oven for 1 hour 10 minutes until a fine skewer inserted into the centre comes out clean. Cool the cake on a wire rack.

PER SLICE 399 kcals, protein 6g, carbs 47g, fat 22g, sat fat 10g, fibre 2g, sugar 31g, salt 0.54g

Any-occasion cake

Whether it's a birthday, Christmas, anniversary or wedding, this gloriously fruity cake will take pride of place. Leave plain, decorate or just squiggle over glacé icing, as here.

TAKES 3 HOURS, PLUS MARINATING
● **CUTS INTO 12 SLICES**

450g/1lb dried mixed fruit
100g/4oz raisins
100g/4oz glacé cherries
grated zest of 1 lemon
grated zest of 1 orange
150ml/¼ pint medium sherry
175g/6oz butter, softened, plus extra
    for greasing
175g/6oz brown soft sugar
100g/4oz plain flour
50g/2oz self-raising flour
50g/2oz ground almonds
1 tsp ground mixed spice
3 eggs

1 Tip the dried fruits and the zests into a bowl, pour over the sherry and leave to marinate overnight. Grease and line a deep 20cm-round cake tin with a double layer of baking parchment. Heat oven to 140C/120C fan/gas 1.

2 Mix all the dry ingredients in a large bowl, together with the butter and eggs. If the mixture starts to curdle, add a little more plain flour. Stir in the fruit, discarding any sherry that has not been absorbed, then spoon the mixture into the tin. Smooth the surface and make a small dip in the middle.

3 Bake in the centre of the oven for 2½ hours until the cake is dark golden brown; an inserted skewer in the centre should come out clean. If the top of the cake browns too quickly, cover it with baking parchment. Leave the cake in the tin for 10 minutes before turning out on to a wire rack to cool.

PER SLICE 414 kcals, protein 5g, carbs 63g, fat 16g, sat fat 8g, fibre 2g, sugar 53g, salt 0.41g

Fabulous fruit & nut cake

This deliciously moist and fruity cake has a syrup, cherry and nut topping – a bit like a Florentine biscuit – which adds a touch of glamour.

TAKES 2½ HOURS • CUTS INTO 12–16 SLICES

FOR THE CAKE

250g/9oz butter, at room temperature, plus extra for greasing

140g/5oz light muscovado sugar

6 eggs, beaten

300g/10oz plain flour

85g/3oz ground almonds

2 tsp each ground ginger and cinnamon

700g/1lb 9oz luxury dried mixed fruit

3 tbsp dark rum

140g/5oz white marzipan, diced

FOR THE TOPPING

50g/2oz each whole skinned hazelnuts and blanched almonds

85g/3oz each brazil nuts and flaked almonds

140g/5oz whole glacé cherries

100g/4oz golden syrup

1 Heat oven to 180C/160C fan/gas 4 and grease and line the base and sides of a deep 20–22cm-round, loose-based cake tin. Beat the butter, sugar, eggs, flour, ground almonds and spices until thoroughly mixed.

2 Measure off 100g/4oz of the cake mixture and set aside. Fold the fruit and rum into the remaining mixture, then gently stir in the marzipan. Spoon this mixture into the cake tin and smooth the surface, making a slight dip in the centre. Bake for 1¼ hours.

3 Mix all the nuts, the cherries and golden syrup into the remaining cake mixture. Spoon this mixture evenly on top of the cake and loosely cover the top of the tin with foil. Return to the oven for 40 minutes more, then take off the foil and bake for another 10–15 minutes so the nuts can turn golden. Insert a skewer into the centre – if it comes out clean, it's ready. Cool in the tin then turn out.

PER SLICE 780 kcals, protein 14g, carbs 95g, fat 40g, sat fat 14g, fibre 4g, sugar 28g, salt 0.67g

Index

Also available from BBC Books and *Good Food*

For 6,000 recipes you can trust see bbcgoodfood.com

bbcgoodfood.com

Great-value family food

Nutty chicken curry

Easy weeknight suppers

Easy sweet & sour chicken

Smart entertaining

Sea bass with sizzled ginger,
chilli & spring onion

Hundreds of desserts

Berry slump

Over 6,000 recipes you can trust